THE POST-QUARANTINE CHURCH

A CHURCH
ANSWERS
RESOURCE

the Post-Quarantine Church

SIX URGENT CHALLENGES + OPPORTUNITIES
That Will Determine the Future of Your Congregation

Thom S. Rainer

TYNDALE
MOMENTUM®

The Tyndale nonfiction imprint

Visit Tyndale online at tyndale.com.

Visit Tyndale Momentum online at tyndalemomentum.com.

TYNDALE, Tyndale's quill logo, *Tyndale Momentum*, and the Tyndale Momentum logo are registered trademarks of Tyndale House Ministries. Tyndale Momentum is the nonfiction imprint of Tyndale House Publishers, Carol Stream, Illinois.

For information about special discounts for bulk purchases, please contact Tyndale House Publishers at csresponse@tyndale.com, or call 1-800-323-9400.

ISBN 978-1-4964-5275-7

Printed in the United States of America

26   25   24   23   22   21   20
7   6   5   4   3   2   1

CONTENTS

AFTER THE QUARANTINE

Do you remember where you were?

It's a common question when talking about historic events. We like to recall exactly where we were and what we were doing when we heard about a great event or a tragic moment. In addition to remembering historic achievements such as landing a man on the moon, tearing down the Berlin Wall, and the Chicago Cubs winning a World Series, I've been around long enough to recall four distinct tragedies, each separated by about twenty years.

Though I was only in third grade at the time, I'll never forget November 22, 1963.

"Boys and girls," my teacher said with a surprising degree of emotion, "I want you all to focus on the words I'm about to say. I want you to remember this moment clearly the rest of your lives. President Kennedy has been shot and killed. He has been assassinated. The president is dead."

That was a hard dose of reality for a classroom of eight-year-olds, but ever since that day, I have been fascinated with the Kennedy assassination. I have my own theories about what happened, and some of my most prized collectibles and artifacts are connected to that sad day.

Fast-forward more than two decades. I was a full-time seminary student, working thirty hours a week at a bank to support my family. I can remember standing in the bank lobby on January 28, 1986, watching on television as the space shuttle *Challenger* lifted off from Cape Canaveral. I remember my confusion when, barely a minute into the flight, the rocket became a ball of fire with plumes of smoke shooting every which way.

It took me about thirty minutes to fully realize the *Challenger* was gone. Seven lives were lost, including that of Christa McAuliffe, the first schoolteacher to go into space.

Fifteen years after the *Challenger* explosion came the tragic event known simply as September 11. I was a seminary dean, and I went to chapel that morning in 2001 with the knowledge that two planes had flown into the twin towers of New York City's World Trade Center. But I didn't know why. By the time chapel was over, the towers had collapsed.

Another two decades later, we were struck by the global coronavirus pandemic, and nation by nation the world went into lockdown mode. Within two months, the unwieldy name for the virus—"2019-nCoV" or "2019 novel coronavirus"— had become "COVID-19" or simply "the virus."

Four tragic moments in history. Four events I will never forget. Four disasters that resulted in death.

But here's the thing about the fourth tragedy. I don't remember where I was when I first heard about COVID-19.

The three previous catastrophes were tied to specific dates and times, but I heard about the virus in bits and pieces. There was no singular event like an assassination, a spaceship explosion, or planes crashing into towers. Our awareness grew only as the virus spread.

The COVID-19 pandemic likely spread to the United States in January 2020. We began to hear about people dying in China and Italy and elsewhere, but few of us were paying attention to the imminent threat to our own nation. The first known COVID-19 deaths in the United States occurred the following month.

I'm not exactly sure when my wife and I began our COVID-19 quarantine. I remember recording podcasts with two guys in my office sometime in March. And I remember one of them saying he was headed home to Kansas City, where he might have to stay for a while because his company was suspending all travel. My self-quarantine would have started shortly after those podcasts, but I don't remember the date with precision.

Here are some other differences I observed: The first three events caused people to flood into churches. The fourth event, the virus, closed the churches' doors for a season. And we knew when the first three events were over, but we're still not entirely certain about the fourth.

I have only the vaguest memory of the Trump administration declaring a public health emergency on January 31, 2020. But I remember the quarantine. I clearly remember the quarantine.

The Quarantined Church

Historians will record the 2020 pandemic from a number of perspectives They will look at the tragedy of widespread death and other health issues. They will point to the state of urgency in hospitals and nursing homes. They will recall the ongoing updates on television and other media, and the daily scorecard that read like a war report: cases confirmed, deaths recorded, and recoveries made.

Stories will certainly be told from an economic standpoint. Companies and stores closing. Some closing permanently. Main streets, malls, and movie theaters emptied. Unemployment soaring. Government assistance and funds flooding forth, encouraging some and frustrating others. Stock markets tanking, then recovering, then becoming unpredictable again.

It will take years before the full emotional and mental toll can be assessed. But it will indeed be a topic of interest for historians, psychologists, counselors, and the news media. We don't know the full story. But we will likely be surprised by how devastating COVID-19 was to the global psyche.

Through my blog, webinars, and church consultations, I walked with tens of thousands of church leaders through the pandemic. I coached many leaders directly and spoke or wrote to nearly a million others. I observed the uncertainty and angst that began when the first in-person worship service was canceled. I witnessed the fallout that followed.

In the early days of the quarantine, I worked with church

leaders primarily on issues of finance and giving. The financial support for many of these churches came primarily through the offering plate. Consequently, with no in-person worship services, there was no offering. With no offering, there were no incoming funds to support the ministries of the church.

As you can imagine, there was an abundance of concern.

I almost wrote, "there was panic," but that would have been misleading and unfair. With few exceptions, there was more faith than fear. More perseverance than panic. These church leaders trusted God wherever he would lead them. But the church leaders were also feeling challenged because they really didn't know where God was leading them.

I guess that's the nature of faith.

As our Church Answers team started working with church leaders on the emerging new realities presented by the lockdown, we focused initially on helping them move as many members as possible to digital giving. We encouraged tech-savvy and highly relational members to work one-on-one with senior adults who had serious apprehensions about the digital world. Then we guided pastors and other church leaders to review their current budgets and planned expenses. What could they postpone? What could they cut? What could they do differently? What could they do better?

Within a few days, we began working with churches to help them move their worship services to a digital format. I was amazed by how energetic and creative most of these members and church leaders were. Though some of the early attempts at streaming their services hit rough spots, they improved with each passing week. The leaders and members knew something was changing, and it was not all bad. More on that later.

I expected to get a lot of questions on pastoral care and reaching the community during the quarantine. Again the church leaders and members surprised me with their drive and innovation. They found ways to minister despite the restrictions imposed by the quarantine. Indeed, many discovered they had a greater outward focus and opportunities for pastoral care than they'd had in previous years. The pandemic, at least as it pertained to serving the surrounding community, was a positive wake-up call.

It felt like forever, but it didn't take long before church leaders were thinking about returning to in-person services. The question wasn't so much *when* they should open. That date varied from community to community and state to state. Rather, they were asking *how* they should open. How do we maintain social distancing in a worship service? Should we add services? Is congregational singing a conduit for the virus? How do we gradually return to in-person gatherings when some people are rarin' to go and others are more reluctant? What do we do with the children? Should we shorten the services?

The questions ranged from numerous to voluminous. At Church Answers, we found ourselves spending more time helping churches get back to in-person services post-quarantine than we had with issues that came up during the quarantine. It was a time of both excitement and concern. Church members and leaders were eager to get back together, but they didn't want to do anything that could be harmful to the well-being of their congregants.

As our team began to walk with churches through the post-quarantine era, I remember my first conversation with a pastor who told me he couldn't wait for things to get back to normal. I responded softly that I didn't think we would *ever* return to the pre-quarantine normal.

I saw the look in his eyes. It was as if I had stolen his joy. His demeanor changed immediately. He could hardly maintain eye contact.

"What do you mean?" he asked sadly.

As much as I hated punching a hole in that pastor's enthusiasm, I didn't want him walking blindly into a world that no longer exists.

As jarring as it may have been for him, I wanted to help him and his church prepare themselves for the post-quarantine era.

"Not So Fast, My Friend!"

I'm a college football fan, and I love watching *College GameDay*'s coverage on ESPN. One of my favorite lines comes from the irrepressible Lee Corso whenever he disagrees with a colleague: "Not so fast, my friend!"

Thus far, I have resisted the temptation to use that line

with church leaders who expect the new normal of the post-quarantine church to look much like the old normal of the pre-pandemic church. Not only will be there be significant differences, but it will also likely take some time before we even begin to understand what the new era will look like.

So, not so fast, my friend!

Allow me instead to share with you what my team and I have learned over the past weeks and months. We have worked with many churches as they've made their reentry to in-person services. There have been some challenges, to be sure, but there have been many more opportunities. We've had the advantage of hearing from thousands of church leaders and members every week. We don't claim to have all the answers, but we have gleaned a lot of good information by asking a lot of questions.

If I could offer some simple advice as we begin, it would be this: *Be excited and encouraged.* Don't let the unknown become a source of fear. You are not entering this new era alone. Not only is God *with* you; he has gone *before* you.

Indeed, as we travel through this book together, I hope you will find cause for optimism and encouragement. My hopeful attitude is based on two realities. First and foremost, none of this—the pandemic, the quarantine, the post-quarantine period—caught God by surprise. He has a plan ready and waiting for his church.

Second, we are already seeing churches adapt and adjust to this season of change in ways unlike any I have seen in my lifetime. I've heard similar themes from pastors, church staff, other church leaders, and church members. They are not entering the post-quarantine era with a business-as-usual mentality. The pandemic was a wake-up call like none other. The post-quarantine era is an opportunity to make the necessary positive changes to move our churches forward.

Get ready to begin the journey. From my perspective, the church is entering the most amazing and exciting days it has seen in decades—maybe even in centuries. Though the path will not always be easy, we can expect future days of great opportunity.

It is time for us to enter this new land of possibilities with hope, promise, and enthusiasm.

Let's begin by discovering new opportunities for the in-person gathered church.

GATHER DIFFERENTLY AND BETTER

Do you remember that simple game we played with our hands as children in Sunday school?

"Here is the church. Here is the steeple. Open the doors and see all the people."

As you opened your hands, if you had intertwined your fingers facing inward, they represented all the people inside the church. It's a fun exercise to show your children or grandchildren.

But the little example became less popular over the years. With theological and biblical precision, people pointed out that the church building is not the church. In fact, some people insisted we stop using the phrase "go to church." They were adamant that people *are* the church; they don't *go* to the church. Like glass-half-empty folks, they seemed to prefer the other version of the "here is the church, here is the steeple" game—the one where you intertwine your fingers on the *outside* of your hands and when you open them up, "Where are all the people?"

Sigh.

Okay, I get it. The church is not a building, and the building is not a church. But the church facility is the place where the church gathers. The church facility may be a traditional church building. It may be a house. It may be a grove of trees. Still, it is a place where the church gathers.

The writer of Hebrews wants church members to encourage and motivate one another. In his letter, he is explicit in this desire and hope: "Let us think of ways to motivate one another to acts of love and good works."[1] So how do we do that? Look at the next verse: "Let us not neglect our meeting together, as some people do, but encourage one another, especially now that the day of his return is drawing near."[2]

Did you get that? As fellow believers, we encourage one another when we meet together. The gathered church is important. Indeed, during the pandemic, we missed the in-person, gathered church greatly.

The quarantine, however, also gave us an opportunity to reflect. As church leaders planned for reentry to the gathered church, they began asking important questions: Are we using our church facilities with optimum stewardship? What can we do differently? What can we do better?

Many church leaders are seeing the post-quarantine era as

a great time to ask these questions. And many are deciding to do things differently.

Simple Church Revisited

When Eric Geiger and I wrote *Simple Church* many years ago, we developed the thesis that churches need a clear plan of discipleship. Based on Eric's research, we discovered that many churches had already developed such a plan, and they communicated their discipleship process through a vision statement.

But we were not fully prepared for the responses we received to *Simple Church*, particularly in one area. One key to being a simple church, we said, was to focus on those areas that were primary to the church's mission and, if possible, eliminate everything else.

Those two words, *focus* and *eliminate*, became rallying cries for many church leaders. Some moved forward with wisdom, eliminating nonessential busywork without creating too much controversy. Some leaders were not so wise. Like the proverbial bull in the china shop, they created more division than efficiency.

Still, the essence of the issue was basic. Our churches had busied themselves trying to do too many things that were not essential to the core mission of the congregation.

Church facilities became the focus of the busy church. We often gauged the health of a congregation by the number of times people came to the facility for worship services, groups, ministries, programs, and events. A busy building, we surmised, was a sign of vibrancy and health.

The unintended consequences of a full church calendar were many. For example, some church members were so busy "going to church" that they failed to be on mission in their community. The most active members were often the least evangelistic members because they spent so much time inside the building instead of out in the community.

Families often suffered as well. Parents had fewer hours for family time because of the steady stream of activities at church. Though the local church was certainly not the only culprit contributing to the overcommitted family, it was a factor for many.

Churches also had challenges with recruiting volunteers. Too many people were too busy. They had no spare time to offer.

Now we have a new opportunity before us. We have seen that the church can survive, even thrive, without the everyday use of buildings. And though we certainly advocate the importance of gathering in person, we also see the opportunity in the post-quarantine era to use our facilities for greater and more efficient purposes.

This brief chapter is by no means an exhaustive compendium of ways to gather better and more efficiently in our facilities. I hope, however, this discussion will stir your creative juices.

When the Community Gathers at Our Facilities

My team and I were doing a consultation for a church that had been experiencing a subtle but noticeable decline for nearly a decade. They wanted outside eyes to look at their congregation. They were in a community with decent demographic growth. They had very nice facilities. They were financially sound. And there had been no major conflicts or controversies in the church.

What could possibly be wrong?

As we do in many of our consultations, we asked for all the documents on the church, both digital and paper. One from this church was particularly fascinating. It was titled "Policies and Procedures for the Use of Church Facilities." It was sixty-four pages long. Seriously.

As our team read this sizable rule book, one thing was very clear: It was a treatise on how to keep the surrounding community *away* from the church.

I understand that churches must have some facility guidelines for coordination and liability purposes. But this manual was ridiculous. It was symptomatic of the inward focus of the congregation. There were too many rules and regulations governing nonmembers. Any guest who was given the document would have received a clear message: *You are not welcome here.*

What if we turned this thinking on its head? What if we

viewed our church facilities as a tool to reach our community? What if we thought of ways to bring the community in instead of keeping them out?

That's a novel concept for many post-quarantine churches.

It's time to reset our perspective in this new era. It's time to reset how we use our facilities. For too many years, church facilities have been primarily for the benefit of *members*. Occasionally, a church would tout the building of a new facility as a way to reach the community. Most of the time, it was an empty promise. As soon as the facility was built, it became simply a new place for church members.

What if we were to look at our church facilities from the perspective of the community? John Mark Clifton tells of his experiences when he began serving as pastor of Wornall Road Baptist Church in Kansas City. The church was on the brink of closing. It had become irrelevant to the community.

The few members left in the congregation saw little hope for their church. Their large facility's deferred maintenance alone seemed an insurmountable barrier to the faithful few. So when the new pastor suggested they get the church ready for the community, it seemed like a major dose of a naiveté or a cruel joke. They were thousands of dollars away from getting their church facilities usable. They could hardly pay their utility bills. How could they possibly revamp their church building for the community?

But the pastor led the endeavor with a few cans of paint and the help of volunteer labor. One room was painted in bright and varied colors. They dubbed it "the birthday room." Then the members put flyers on their neighbors' doors. The message was simple but compelling. The church would provide a place for neighborhood children to celebrate birthdays. The cost would be zero. Church members would assist at the parties. The only thing the neighbor had to do was make a reservation and show up with the kids.

It was transformative—not only for the families in the neighborhood; it was transformative for the church.

Typically, churches will welcome the community for well-planned, seasonal events. The Christmas musical. The Easter presentation. The children's concert. And there's nothing wrong with these events. But what if we tried something different? What if we *asked the community* how our church facilities could best serve them? What if we turned the purpose of our church buildings upside down? What if the facilities became a place *for* the community as well as a place *in* the community?

During the quarantine, many church leaders and church members discovered that the church was still the church, even without its facilities. Yes, we desired to return to in-person gatherings so we could be with our friends again. But we found we could do a lot of things as a church without relying on our buildings. Indeed, the digital world opened up possibilities that many congregations had never considered, much less tried.

We realized, it seemed, that our facilities were more tools than necessities. What if we now use those tools to reach and minister to our community?

I recently took a tour of a church facility in Georgia that had been remodeled to better minister to the community. Nearly half of the large buildings were now dedicated specifically to community needs. One section was a large break area for law enforcement. Another area was used as a medical clinic. By the time they were done, the building included numerous washers and dryers that community residents could use at no cost. During certain hours, childcare was provided at the church laundromat.

Another church in a different economic demographic began making plans to establish partnerships with local businesses. They already had a place for community members to work with free Wi-Fi. But they wanted to do more. When they heard about other churches that have sandwich shops and restaurants on-site owned by for-profit businesses, and one that opened its facilities to a private preschool instead of recreating the wheel by starting their own preschool ministry, they were inspired to take a blank slate approach and think creatively about their options. I'm certain this church will soon become a magnet *in* and *for* their community.

The leaders of a rural church, located in a sparsely populated area with nothing resembling a community center for thirty miles, are now dreaming about using their worship center and fellowship hall for community needs. They realize that the small school in the area doesn't have an adequate space to hold events. But the church's worship center can hold nearly two hundred people. It is ideal for community *and* school events.

Do you get the picture? Having become accustomed to doing without our buildings for many weeks, we're now able to look at our church facilities with different eyes. We can see them more as a tool for outreach rather than a cocoon for members.

Churches across America and around the world own billions of dollars' worth of real estate and facilities. God has provided these assets for us to be good stewards. Most church facilities go unused for large blocks of time every week. It's time to rethink our facilities. It's time to open them up to our communities.

A New Mindset: Looking for Signs

I have led or participated in hundreds of church consultations. One of the first things our consulting team does on-site is take a tour of the church facilities. We look at the parking area. We do a quick assessment of the worship-center capacity. We focus on the children's area for safety and hygiene. We ask about the flow of both automobile traffic and foot traffic.

Among our many checkpoints is an inventory of the signs in and around the church buildings. Is there good directional signage entering the parking lot? Can visitors easily locate the main entrance to the church building? Are restrooms clearly marked? Are young parents able to see on their first visit where to take their children?

Over the years, we have mentally noted and sometimes written about "*un*welcome signs." These are the signs that tell members and guests (usually guests) what they *can't* do. Don't bring coffee into the sanctuary. Don't enter the worship service after 11:15 a.m. Don't loiter in the parking lot. No skateboards.

You get the idea.

While some of these signs are there for safety and liability purposes, most have been posted to keep outsiders from messing up the church property. The signs are an outward, physical expression of an inwardly focused church. The church facility is an exclusive haven for church members. Don't disturb the religious club or any of its artifacts.

The post-quarantine church has a new opportunity because God has given us a way to see our church facilities in a new light. We learned that it isn't absolutely necessary to have millions of dollars in facilities in order to have a church. But maybe, just maybe, since so many of us already have these facilities in place, God intends for us to use them for the good of our communities.

We may have to do some extra cleaning and paint the walls more often. But that's a small price to pay to reach people all around us with the lifesaving gospel of Jesus.

Open the Doors More Often

My conversation with a pastor from Virginia was insightful. His church had never livestreamed their services before the pandemic. Like other leaders, he jumped into the digital world out of necessity.

"We couldn't meet in person, so we had to meet virtually," he told me. "But our church is not that big; we had never tried Facebook Live or anything like it. We had to learn quickly. It was rough at first, but we caught on pretty well."

While other pastors and church leaders were excited about the number of Facebook views they were getting early in the quarantine, this Virginia pastor was not enamored. "Intuitively, I just didn't put much stock in the number of people who may have watched us for three seconds or thirty seconds. It was almost like a passing fad."

What fascinated me about our conversation, however, was his totally different perspective of the streaming process, at least compared to most of his peers.

"While my pastor buddies were getting excited about views, I noticed something else taking place," he said. "My church members began sharing with me the different days or times when they watched the services. I heard the same thing from a number of people in the community."

By the intensity on his face, I could see his mind working. "It was a big lesson for me," he continued with even more enthusiasm. "People were 'attending' our services at different times and different days. Before COVID-19, we were thinking we would have to add a second Sunday morning service. Not anymore. We have this nice-size facility that hardly ever gets used except about two days a week. If people are watching us digitally at different times, maybe they would like to have different options for days to attend an in-person service."

The pastor began testing Thursday nights as a possibility. So far, he is encouraged by the response. He heard our Church Answers team say that about one-third of the American workforce is at work on Sundays, and he really wants to reach that group in his community.

It only took a pandemic and some rethinking about the use of his church facilities to move him in that direction.

Two (or More) Churches, One Location

The past two decades have witnessed the rapid growth of multisite churches. In the early days of this movement, these churches often described themselves as "one church, two locations." This phenomenon shows no signs of slowing. The multisite movement was once solely the domain of larger churches. Today, churches of all sizes may have more than one location.

A church planter who is part of our Church Answers community shared a story about a providential digital meeting with another member of the community. Members often have conversations at our forum called Church Answers Central.

"We were commenting about the timing of reopening," he began. "I shared that our situation was particularly challenging because we had been meeting at a local middle school, and the school would not open for our church anytime soon."

Somehow, one of the pastors in the forum recognized that the church planter was in his same community. "It was an incredible moment," the young church planter told us. "He messaged me and we began a conversation. That led to several phone calls, and he eventually invited us to share his church facility. For now, we will meet on Sunday afternoon, at least until we can find a better option. And we really had *no* options until we connected."

The quarantine was a challenge. The quarantine was also a blessing.

Pastors and other church leaders began to view their times of gathering with fresh eyes. Likewise, they began to view their facilities with a fresh perspective. The post-quarantine era may prove to be a time of extraordinary experimentation and innovation in the use of church facilities.

At the very least, we hope many churches will become much more intentional about using their church facilities as a means to connect with their communities. We agree that the building is not the church, but it can be a valuable tool.

We hope many churches will welcome schools, businesses, and local governments to use their facilities. In some smaller communities, the church facility may be the closest thing they have to a community center.

We hope many churches will use their facilities for gathered worship services at new and innovative times; that they will not be stuck in old paradigms that make no sense from a stewardship perspective.

We hope some different churches will meet in the same facilities. There is usually plenty of room and plenty of available days for other congregations.

Because churches could not gather for a season, they are now learning how to gather both differently and better. As a happy consequence, both the churches and their communities will be healthier and served more vibrantly.

Three Thoughts

1. Think of one innovative way your church could use its facilities, perhaps something that has never been done.

2. Think of alternative days and times when your church could gather for worship services. Think creatively to reach people you are not currently reaching.

3. Think of ways your church could possibly partner with the local government or schools to use your facilities.

SEIZE YOUR OPPORTUNITY TO REACH THE DIGITAL WORLD

The COVID-19 pandemic is a historical marker for numerous reasons. The very fact that a deadly virus gripped the entire world is reason enough. Not since the 1918 influenza known as the Spanish flu has the world experienced such a widespread epidemic of infectious disease.

We all know some of the major consequences of COVID-19. Millions of people were infected. Hundreds of thousands died. The global economy was put to the test. In local communities in the US, scores of businesses were deeply harmed; some closed altogether. It will take years to fully grasp the emotional and psychological damage inflicted upon millions of people worldwide.

Yet we also know that many people and organizations saw opportunities and benefited from the pandemic. Some big technology companies, for example, were flush with cash during the pandemic as several of their business lines did well. They used the cash to buy back shares of their own stock and to acquire smaller companies, many of which needed a quick infusion of liquidity to survive.[1]

It's still too early to fully assess the impact of the pandemic—both positive and negative—on churches. But I watched in amazement as many church leaders adapted very well during the quarantine. The most visible adjustment was the streaming of worship services.

I don't think we have yet grasped how significant this adjustment was for a great majority of church leaders and members. We had seen larger churches stream their services for years. But based on results from our initial surveys, we estimate that more than 100,000 churches that had never had an internet presence beyond a website began streaming their worship services during the pandemic. And more than 250,000 congregations had never had a digital presence of any kind before the quarantine. Our numbers are broad estimates but nonetheless mind-boggling.

As the internet increasingly became a conduit for the gospel, for biblical teaching, and for ministry across North America churches of all sizes began to discover a new mission field in the digital world. Every week, we heard from pastors and other church leaders about people becoming followers of Christ, restoring marriages and other relationships, and connecting to a church for the first time ever—all through initial contacts made in the digital realm.

Yes, there have been challenges, but at the same time, it seems some amazing opportunities are unfolding—at least from my perspective. Time and again, churches are demonstrating their resilience and their determination to see how God will work for the good of his overall purpose through this devastating disease.

As the post-quarantine era began, churches expanded their thinking and moved into new territories. We heard leaders asking the right question: How do we move forward most effectively in these uncharted waters? Though they could see the potential mission field of the digital world, most admitted they were not certain how best to reach people and minister to them in this new context. Their questions were not simply about navigating unfamiliar technologies, but about how best to move forward on all fronts. This new era will likely include some blending and balancing between digital and in-person ministry.

How Has Digital Ministry Changed in the Post-Quarantine Era?

For certain, a few churches were rethinking their digital presence long before the pandemic and the resulting quarantine. And there were clearly defined differences between these forward-thinking churches and other congregations. Most congregations still viewed the digital world, at most, as a tool and an extension of the "normal" ministries of the church. But for forward-thinking churches, the digital world was already a mission field—a largely untapped area for local church ministry.

The post-quarantine church is more likely to grasp the perspectives of these innovative churches. During the quarantine, they not only discovered ways to continue their existing ministries, but they also began to see new fields and new opportunities.

In the pre-pandemic world, a gradual migration of churches toward the use of digital tools was already underway. Churches with an online presence typically had a website to provide information about the church—service times, locations, staff profiles, a statement of faith, and various other facts. Some churches used social media to communicate to members and, perhaps, to the community. Whether through Facebook, Instagram, Twitter, or some other platform, a small but significant number of churches used social media to communicate on a regular basis. Some congregations even used social media as a key part of their outreach strategy.

A relatively small but growing number of churches were active in the digital world through specific email and text messaging strategies. Their digital outreach was both focused and strategic.

My point in giving this brief overview of digital ministry before the pandemic is to remind us that it is not something exclusive to the post-quarantine church. The same digital tools that were being used before are still being used today, but now those tools are being used more vigorously and enthusiastically.

What has changed is the perspective of the digital world among church leaders and members. Many more are now embracing the attitudes of the forward-thinking early adopters—namely that the digital world is only secondarily a tool; it is primarily a mission field. As we move into the post-quarantine church era, the challenge is how best to reach people and serve them on the digital mission field.

So that leaves us with some questions. If we see this new era as an opportunity to reach a new mission field, what does that mean for church practices? How do we think differently? How do we respond differently? How will our church members respond if we begin to make the necessary changes to move forward in this new era?

What are some early lessons we are learning in this post-quarantine world?

We certainly do not have all the information we would like, but we still must begin the process. As we move through the rest of this chapter, I hope we can begin to understand the post-quarantine church in its infancy.

The opportunities are too important to ignore.

A Plan to Begin Reaching the Digital World

The early days of the quarantine were often filled with concern and confusion for church leaders. What are we going to do if we can't gather in person? How can we make sure our church is sufficiently funded? How will we minister to people we can't see in person? What do we do about our small groups?

The initial period of question upon question transitioned to a level of excitement as church leaders and members discovered the possibilities in the digital world. To be clear, they had been aware of this world (to varying degrees), but now they were seeing it with fresh eyes.

The immediate challenge, however, of now viewing the digital world as a mission field is that missionaries typically have *a plan* in place before they venture into a new field. For most church leaders, the effects of the pandemic were unexpected and sudden. Pastors and other leaders were unprepared and often confused about what to do next. Simply stated, they had no plan for this disruption. So the initial wave of questions and confusion followed by excitement soon led to more questions and confusion.

Before the pandemic, most church leaders were not concerned about reaching people in the digital world. They focused their attention on the opportunities available in person. After all, that was the mission field they knew and where they had been all their lives. That was the mission field for which they were trained.

But now things are different. Very different.

As church leaders finally began to think more seriously about reaching the digital world, restrictions eased in their communities and it became time to plan their reentry into the in-person world. Most leaders were consumed with physical preparations to reopen and making certain they took into consideration all the warnings and safety precautions.

But many of these church leaders and members had not forgotten their desire to reach people digitally. They had caught a glimpse of the opportunities during the pandemic, and now they wanted their post-quarantine church to make some bold moves. There was an intensified desire to move into this new mission field.

Perhaps you're among them and you're wondering what to do next. While once again acknowledging that it's early in the post-quarantine era, and though we're cautious about making definitive declarations, we can see some promising plans beginning to unfold.

At the core of many of these plans is a realization that churches must deal with three groups: what we're calling *digital only*, *digitally transitioning*, and *dual citizens*.

The first group represents a digital-only presence, which could include people who are physically unable to attend in-person gatherings. They could be anyone from elderly shut-ins to members of the armed forces stationed overseas.

The digital-only group also includes people who may still consider it too risky to enter a church's physical facilities because of COVID-19, and some who are simply unwilling or unready to attend a church service. They are not totally antichurch, but they're not eager to gather with the in-person fellowship. Some may be willing to make that transition in the future; some may never take a step further. How will churches reach and minister to these people?

The second group are digitally transitioning people. They are still mostly connected to the church digitally. They rarely, if ever, attend an in-person gathering. But there are indications they are somewhat open to connecting in person. Perhaps they've joined a video-based small group and have begun to get to know others better. Perhaps they completed a digital connection card during a streaming service. A strategy to reach out to these people may include specific ways to encourage them to attend an in-person worship service.

The third group are the dual citizens. They are connected to your congregation both digitally and in person. This distinction is important to remember. It's pretty rare anymore to find someone who has *no* digital connections, even if they strongly prefer in-person gatherings. Most people in North America have some level of digital presence. Indeed, I just liked a Facebook post by my eighty-four-year-old mother-in-law.

The future strategy for churches, therefore, must keep in mind these three groups.

So where do we begin?

Lessons on Prayer from the Early Church

Interestingly, the experience of the early church in Jerusalem is instructive for our forays into the digital world today. Though the means of communication were quite different, the need for faith was not.

Shortly before Jesus ascended to heaven, he told his followers, "You will receive power when the Holy Spirit comes upon you. And you will be my witnesses, telling people about me everywhere—in Jerusalem, throughout Judea, in Samaria, and to the ends of the earth."[2]

That was it. No other instructions. No strategic plan. No further clarity of purpose.

So what did they do when they didn't know what to do?

They prayed.

The Bible indicates that the prayers of the early church were powerful because the people were of one mind: "They all met together and were constantly united in prayer."[3]

They didn't know what else to do, but they knew they were supposed to pray.

It's easy to become fascinated by the technological possibilities of this newly discovered digital mission field. But we must not allow them to undermine our commitment to prayer and seeking God's guidance. It's an exercise in futility to try to reach and minister to the digital world without prayer as a first step. It's like trying to accomplish God's mission without God.

Though we are not offering specific methodologies to guide your church in prayer, we strongly recommend that you keep in mind the three major groups we're trying to reach in the post-quarantine era: digital only, digitally transitioning, and dual citizens.

How will you pray for each of these groups? What ways will you make available for the primarily digital groups to share prayer needs with you? How will you involve the dual citizens in praying for the other groups? How will your church leaders and members maintain an active and vibrant prayer ministry in the post-quarantine era?

It's an exciting time. But if we attempt to move forward without prayer, the opportunity will quickly devolve from God-empowered to human-centered. The latter is a guarantee for failure.

The Digital Simple Church

In *Simple Church*, Eric Geiger and I highlighted effective churches that had developed a clear process of discipleship. One of the key steps for these churches was to focus on doing a few things well and eliminate everything else, if possible.

As we prayerfully seek ways for our churches to become a more potent missional force in the digital world, we must be careful not to fall into the trap of church busyness. God has uniquely equipped each of our congregations to move forward in the post-quarantine era. But we can't do everything.

To state it more imperatively, we *must not* attempt to do everything.

We will be tempted to try all the latest technological add-ons for our streaming services. The creativity is already flowing. You will no doubt hear about churches that are trying new features and experiencing great results. Though we certainly should be open to new ideas and applications, we cannot implement all of them. Indeed, if we overreach by jumping into several areas at once, we will dilute our effectiveness in most of them.

Post-quarantine churches will be present on the various social media channels. There are many who are already pointing us to more effective strategies on Facebook. Others are saying we must be strategic on Twitter to disseminate pithy information about our churches. Still others advocate the necessity of an active YouTube channel for congregations. I recently heard from one group that was telling churches they would become irrelevant if they were not strategically moving forward with Instagram. Or Pinterest. Or LinkedIn. Or whatever flavor is next.

I recently saw a tutorial for churches in the digital world. It featured more than *forty* social media channels. I was exhausted just reading the summary article.

I love the enthusiasm of churches trying to discover ways to be more effective on the digital mission field. But the same pitfalls they needed to avoid in the pre-quarantine era are still out there, though perhaps in different forms. The means can become the end. Busyness can replace effectiveness. Activity can eclipse results.

My team and I have worked with thousands of churches. We have a consistent message: Don't get so busy with programs, ministries, and activities that you miss the original intent of these efforts. They are meant to fulfill the Great Commission and the Great Commandment. Their purpose is not to fill a spot on a calendar.

We are already seeing tendencies toward digital busyness

in post-quarantine churches. For many leaders, FOMO (fear of missing out) is real and present. Your church must indeed be a missional force in the digital world. But it can't do everything. It can't be on every social media channel. It can't have every new feature in its streaming worship services. It can't be digitally omnipresent.

Find those areas in the digital world where your church can do a few things well. Put your efforts and focus in those areas. Don't be lured by the temptations of digital busyness or digital noise. Regularly and ruthlessly evaluate your church's effectiveness, and make shifts when needed.

Whatever you do, don't confuse busyness with effectiveness in the digital world. It is usually just the opposite.

The Both/And World

The post-quarantine world will no doubt include churches that move to the extremes of the in-person and digital spectrum. Some congregations will become so enamored of the digital mission field that they'll forget the vital importance of in-person gatherings. They may lose focus on providing a great preaching and worship experience for the gathered church. They may lose sight of the healthy ways in which many in-person groups can flourish.

On the other end of the spectrum, some congregations will assume that the post-quarantine church will be just like the pre-quarantine church. Their focus is on "getting back to normal." During the peak of the pandemic, these church leaders and members could not wait until everyone could return to the way things used to be—resuming old programs, old methods, and old activities.

The biggest problem with the "back to normal" approach is that the world has changed significantly. The pre-quarantine world and post-quarantine world are not the same. Churches cannot minister effectively using methods for a world that no longer exists.

Another mistake we can make is to assume that moving into the digital world is just one more activity. Many of our churches rightly discovered that the digital world is now part of our mission field. Their eyes were opened to new and exciting opportunities. But as we move forward in the post-quarantine era, we must think of our community and our mission field as *both/and*, not *either/or*. There will be no one-size-fits-all strategy; it will differ from church to church. The common denominator for most churches will still be in-person worship services. But the types and frequency of digital streaming services will vary from one congregation to the next.

There will be differences as well in the approach to groups. Some churches found success with digital groups during the quarantine and will continue some form of them in the future. Others will use digital delivery for short-term groups only, favoring in-person gatherings for ongoing groups.

Undoubtedly, there will be a great deal of innovation in how churches reach people and minister to them in the digital world, especially with those who are not connected to an in-person gathering. For now, the situation and strategies are fluid. And they will likely remain that way for the next several years.

What is most important as an underlying principle is our commitment to obey the Great Commission. We know that the world is both digital and physical. For that reason alone, our churches must respond to both. And though the ways we reach these two mission fields will vary and change, it is imperative that we do something and do it well. Waiting is not an option.

"The harvest is great, but the workers are few. So pray to the Lord who is in charge of the harvest; ask him to send more workers into his fields."[4]

Three Thoughts

1. Think of the differences in your community since the pandemic and the implications for how you will do ministry in this new era.

2. Think of which social media channels might be most effective for your church now.

3. Think of how your church could connect best with a non-Christian who has only a digital connection to your church.

RECONNECT WITH THE COMMUNITY NEAR YOUR CHURCH

I remember the good old days.

As I study the development and path of local churches in America, I have concluded the good old days really were good, not just memories of my wishful thinking.

In the past two centuries, about eight out of ten churches were started in and for a specific community. There were also county seat churches, whose congregations came from more than one neighborhood or area. Similarly, there were large urban churches, whose draw often extended to ten or twenty miles.

Most churches, however, were founded as part of a specific neighborhood or community. Churches often bore the name of their community or of a well-traveled street in the community. The people who attended these churches lived in the neighborhood. The church clearly reflected the community's identity.

I do remember the good old days.

I became a follower of Christ when I was a teenager. But the church I attended was in turmoil. I have terrible memories of bitter church business meetings where vitriolic accusations were hurled from one church member to another. The church ended up splitting, and my family chose the side of those who left the congregation.

It didn't take long, however, before our splinter church went through another battle, resulting in yet a third church. Though I take full responsibility for failing to connect with a congregation as a new Christian, I decided I couldn't be a part of any of the three churches. So I stopped attending church when I was a young teenager.

Disconnected Christians do not do well, and I was no exception. Instead of growing from the point of my new-found faith, I reverted to rebellious behavior. I became more disillusioned than discipled.

Fast-forward to the first two years of my marriage as a young twentysomething. My wife had one major request of me as we contemplated starting a family. She wanted to find a church home. She wanted me to be not only a family leader but also a spiritual leader. I was somewhat surprised by how eager I was to comply.

Getting connected to a church was a suppressed longing I'd had for years. I approached the opportunity to join a congregation with enthusiasm. We soon found a church home. The church was in our community and clearly identified with the community by name.

Those days were truly good old days. I attribute much of my early spiritual growth to the accountability and love I experienced in that local church. Much of our life together revolved around the church and the neighborhood where we lived. When our first child was born, we became an active family of three in the church.

Community churches and neighborhood churches have long been a major component of our nation's heritage and life. It was just natural and common for the church to care for those who lived in the community.

Many of these neighborhood churches, however, forgot their purpose over time. For some congregations, when the neighborhood changed, the church did not change with it. In other churches, the congregation became inwardly focused and became more like a religious social club than a church. Still others failed to remain relevant to new generations, and those generations either moved to a newer and larger church or dropped out of church altogether.

In more recent days, when the COVID-19 pandemic forced churches to close the doors of their facilities, an interesting transformation took place in many congregations. They began to rediscover their communities.

Rediscovering Our Church Address

During the quarantine, we were regularly reminded by church leaders and church members that the church wasn't *closed*. Certainly, from a biblical perspective, the admonitions were correct. As many people reminded us on blogs, Facebook, and other media, the church is the people, not the buildings.

Got it.

Still, something wonderfully ironic transpired during the pandemic. Churches became more people-oriented as their freedom to gather people together was taken away. There were at least four reasons this transformation happened.

First, because most of their activities had taken place in the church building, churches were no longer activity-driven. With their facilities closed, congregations had more time and opportunity to focus beyond themselves. And guess what? Many churches found a community eager to engage with them. Many churches found people in the neighborhood who were longing for a connection with the church whose familiar building they knew but whose people they did not often encounter.

Second, a number of congregations renewed or began prayer ministries, some of which focused intentionally on their neighborhoods and communities. One church we observed spent a few dollars on Facebook ads targeting their community by zip code. Then they spent time interacting on a community Facebook page. In both cases, they offered prayer for anyone who asked. They gave a specific email address for submitting prayer requests.

The community's response exceeded everyone's expectations in the church. Many members confessed they had never thought about reaching out to neighbors and community members until the prayer ministry began.

Third, during the quarantine, many churches became more intentional about evangelism. This is indeed ironic—evangelizing more when you cannot be physically present with others. But it makes sense if we keep in mind our first point about busyness. Church leaders and church members were freed from a laundry list of activities. They could focus on the things that really mattered, such as sharing the gospel with people in the community.

The fourth issue is also ironic. Because so many people were largely confined to their homes and their immediate neighborhoods, they saw *more* of their neighbors as they walked, rode their bikes, or sat on the porch. Even while maintaining good social distancing, they were close enough to say hello or carry on a conversation. Church members had opportunities to connect with neighbors that maybe they had never met.

So what are the lessons of the quarantine for the post-quarantine era? Perhaps one of the most powerful and poignant things we've learned is to remember that our churches are in the community for a reason. As Church Answers president Sam Rainer often reminds us, "Your church address is no accident." Most churches' physical location should also be the hub of their ministry.

As we move into the post-quarantine era, churches should remember the four key lessons they learned about community during the quarantine. These lessons are powerful reminders of the importance of people, prayer, and purpose in our post-quarantine ministry.

Keep church life simple, not so busy with activities that the members can't do the most important ministries they are supposed to be doing.

Make certain your congregation's prayer ministry engages with your community or neighborhood. Become a hub of prayer for the homes in your area.

Be intentional about sharing the gospel. *That* you do it is far more important than *how* you do it.

Finally, keep the emphasis on having your members connect with people in the community.

Great new efforts on behalf of the gospel emerged during the pandemic and quarantine. There's no reason they shouldn't continue in the post-quarantine era.

The Power of Asking *and* Listening

"Never again!"

That exclamation came from a pastor in the fourth week of self-quarantine. The pandemic for him, as for many others, was a time of reflection. He was in his eighth year as pastor at his church. By his own admission, he had lost the focus he once had.

"I came to this church after planting another church," he shared with me in a coaching call. "I approached ministry at my current church with the same fervor and strategy as my church plant. I led my church to reach out to the community every way possible. One church member jokingly said we were 'community obsessed.' I liked that phrase."

He paused for a moment and I could tell he was recalling those days fondly. "Thom, you know how you say that we church leaders often let the good replace the great in our ministries?" I told him I did, and he continued, "Well, that's what happened to me. I particularly stopped spending as much time leading our church to reach our community. We got busy doing other stuff. Not *bad* stuff. Just *other* stuff."

He repeated his earlier words: "Never again!"

For a number of reasons, church leaders and church members became community focused during the pandemic. For my pastor friend, he had time to reflect on the direction his church had taken. It gave him an opportunity to make course adjustments.

Others said they noticed an eagerness in the community to engage churches and their members. Maybe the pandemic reminded people of their mortality. Or they desired prayer. Or they wanted connection. Whatever it was, they were much more receptive to the local congregation.

The post-quarantine era is the perfect time to reset,

particularly in the ways we connect with our communities or neighborhoods. In a variety of ways, church leaders are saying, "Never again!" Here are some simple but powerful examples.

A church in Tennessee bought thousands of dollars in small gift cards from local merchants. They told each business owner they wanted to pray for him or her and support small businesses in the community. Many of the merchants were moved to tears. This church knows that the relationships they started during the pandemic will grow in the post-quarantine days. They do not intend to slow down in reaching out to local businesses.

A church in Missouri opened its large fellowship hall to the community. It's available for family reunions, birthday parties, meetings for local businesses, and receptions. The idea was conceived during the pandemic and birthed in the post-quarantine era. The only charge is a modest amount for cleaning. Even then, the church is willing to help those who cannot afford the cleaning fee.

As noted earlier, a church in Georgia turned a portion of their facilities into a free laundromat for community residents. Many of the people who use the washers and dryers leave their unused laundry detergent for those who follow. For three hours on three different evenings, the church provides childcare while parents or grandparents use the laundromat.

How did these and other churches decide on opportunities to connect better with their communities? The process was simple but profound. They asked people in the community how the church could best help them. And then they listened.

One church called more than one hundred merchants and community leaders during the quarantine. They now have a powerful road map of plans to use for connecting with the community moving forward. Another church sent handwritten letters to the residents of more than eight hundred homes in the community. They provided an email address for prayer requests. Within one week, 134 people had responded. That church now has a much clearer picture of the needs in their community. And they have a clearer path forward.

The churches asked. The churches listened. The churches acted.

These actions are but a few examples of how churches viewed the quarantine and post-quarantine as windows of opportunity. For these churches, the opportunities God provided during the pandemic will likely be extended for years to come.

The Principle of Slow Erosion

I love Florida beaches. I have been going to beaches on the Panhandle or in southwest Florida all my life. The sugar-white sand and emerald water make for some of the most beautiful landscapes I have ever seen.

Beaches are part of a delicate ecosystem. Many are in a

constant state of erosion. More often than not, the erosion is subtle, hardly noticeable month by month or even year by year. Beach residents rarely raise concerns about the slow erosion.

When a hurricane hits the beaches, however, the erosion is usually significant and dramatic. Residents and local officials move into urgency mode. After property damage is assessed and repaired, beach restoration follows. The urgency moves many people to action.

In the church, the slow erosion in most congregations was tied to the drift in their outward focus. Most churches had begun using their resources of time, people, ministries, and money to take care of themselves. It was a gradual process. It was not as if church leaders and members decided one day they would cut back their efforts to reach the community.

It was more of a year-by-year process of replacing the Great Commission with a great complacency. As the church turned inward, its connections to the community gradually washed away.

Jesus gave the first church in Jerusalem a clear command to be outwardly focused—beginning in the city itself and then spreading "throughout Judea, in Samaria, and to the ends of the earth."[1] The church did well in its early days in Jerusalem. Their outward focus on the community was powerful and pervasive. But the church was not fully obedient. The gospel was meant to go beyond Jerusalem. The church stopped at the edge of its comfort zone.

God then allowed persecution to create a sense of urgency for the Jerusalem church, while at the same time igniting the next phase of the Great Commission.

> A great wave of persecution began that day, sweeping over the church in Jerusalem; and all the believers except the apostles were scattered through the regions of Judea and Samaria.[2]

In our day, God has sent a wave of urgency to the world in the form of COVID-19. It is clearly and powerfully a wake-up call. For most congregations, it is not a matter of getting *beyond* Jerusalem—that is, going beyond the borders of our local communities. It is first a matter of *reaching* Jerusalem. We must focus our outward vision on the people who are right around us, in our neighborhoods, cities, and towns.

For the most part, churches have seen their outward focus slowly erode. We may not have noticed it clearly before the quarantine. But we're certainly aware of it in these post-quarantine days.

The challenge has been laid. We cannot and must not return to the days of comfort and routine. We must move forward with Great Commission obedience and sacrifice.

The pastor I quoted earlier was right. His words were on target.

Never again!

The Return of the Neighborhood Church

I have been in many types of churches. The first church I served as pastor was a rural congregation of seven people. The nearest store of any kind was fifteen miles away. At the other end of the spectrum, I have been part of large, regional churches with congregants coming from many miles away. As a child, I grew up in a small-town, county seat church.

Each of these churches made a major contribution to my spiritual growth. Each congregation became an integral part of my family life and health. I am grateful to God for the churches that have meant so much to me. To this day, my adult sons and I recall with gratitude the shaping influence of the churches in their lives when they were children.

One particular type of church that is experiencing a comeback in areas around the world is the neighborhood church. Though there are various definitions of this category, most have key similarities.

The most common characteristic of a neighborhood church is its geographical specificity. These churches were originally started to serve a very precise area, self-identified by the residents as a unique and distinctive community. When residents were asked where they lived, they had a clear geographical response.

Sometimes the area was a subdivision, with a specific name. In other neighborhoods, the identifying geographical marker was a major employer.

Neighborhood churches were started *in* a community *for* the community. Their purpose was clear. Their geographical mission field was precisely defined.

Neighborhood churches have not fared well for the past few decades. It is not uncommon to blame their decline on larger churches, specifically megachurches. But the wounds were largely self-inflicted. Some neighborhood churches became magnet churches based on a denominational distinction rather than a geographical location. Instead of adapting to a changing population, church members moved out of the neighborhood and drove miles to church. When the church membership demographic is significantly different from the community's, that church is already on a path toward decline.

Some neighborhood churches became inwardly focused. They were originally founded to reach and minister to the community, but over time they became a religious social club. They began to serve themselves instead of serving others.

Similarly, other neighborhood churches became irrelevant. They resisted change for no other reason than to maintain the status quo. When younger members left the neighborhood church for a larger church, it was not always simply to go to a bigger place. These young families often moved to a more relevant congregation. They grew weary of the battles to resist change in the old neighborhood church. Today, many neighborhood churches are making a comeback. Some are stand-alone congregations. Others are campuses of a larger church. Their mission, however, is the same. They are *in* the community, *of* the community, and *for* the community.

Potentially, one of the more positive outcomes of the pandemic will be the accelerated comeback of neighborhood churches. We were already seeing signs of this turnaround before COVID-19. Now, with the wisdom, insight, and inspiration gained during the quarantine, we are even more hopeful about the post-quarantine church.

The comeback of the neighborhood church is part of a larger trend. Churches are reconnecting with their communities. Congregations are discovering they cannot exist as a meaningful extension of Christ's ministry if they are focused exclusively on themselves.

The revival of neighborhood churches in particular and the renewed focus of congregations on their communities in general are exciting developments. Indeed, we see the likelihood that these trends will not only continue but also accelerate in the months to come.

The result will be healthier churches. The result will also be healthier communities. God is truly using a challenging and tragic time to bring things together for his glory.

Three Thoughts

1. Think of some ways your church can be more of a positive influence in the community.

2. Think about the principle of slow erosion, and consider whether this gradual decline is taking place in your church.

3. Think about the comeback of the neighborhood church, and consider whether some of those positive developments are in place in your congregation.

TAKE PRAYER TO A NEW AND POWERFUL LEVEL

I wish I prayed as much as I talk and write about prayer.

Seriously.

Cognitively, I know prayer is foundational to the health of a church. I know that any efforts of a church without prayer are human-centered and ultimately destined for failure. I know empirically that the healthiest churches are those with a high priority on prayer.

But I struggle in my personal prayer life more often than I care to admit. When I served as a pastor, I emphasized prayer more eagerly to my congregation than I spent time in prayer.

I was often too busy with church activities to spend time with God. Sadly, I still struggle with praying consistently.

Many pastors I coach have confided similar struggles. In

their church lives, they have been too busy with the tyranny of the urgent to spend much time in prayer.

But something happened during the pandemic and the quarantine. Pastors and other church leaders began to seek God in prayer more fervently. Church members became more involved in prayer ministries. In many cases, residents in the community began contacting churches for prayer support.

Church history is replete with examples of the ebbs and flows of prayer movements. Consider, for example, the first church in Jerusalem. The church was born from a movement of prayer after Christ's ascension: "They all met together and were constantly united in prayer, along with Mary the mother of Jesus, several other women, and the brothers of Jesus."[1]

Notice in that one brief verse the priority of prayer. They *all* met together. No exceptions. Even Mary, the mother of Jesus, was a part of the prayer movement.

Notice as well the *frequency* of their prayer. Luke, the author of Acts, says it was *constant*. Though we don't know much more about their meetings than that, the message is pretty straightforward: Prayer was important.

Not only was prayer important—it was also a unifying force in the church. The believers who gathered for prayer were of one heart and one mind.

After Pentecost, the Jerusalem church began to take shape. We see the immediate priorities of the nascent congregation in Acts 2:42: "All the believers devoted themselves to the apostles' teaching, and to fellowship, and to sharing in meals (including the Lord's Supper), and to prayer." The mention of prayer at the end of the list of priorities could be an indication that it was the pinnacle of importance. The church *devoted* themselves to prayer. Prayer was not a mere formality or a routine ministry. It was such a priority that it consumed the members of the first church. The power of this congregation would be not human centered; it would be God directed.

Shortly before persecution scattered the church beyond Jerusalem, the early leaders dealt with a ministry challenge. There was a divide between the Greek-speaking believers and the Hebrew-speaking believers over the distribution of food to the widows. Those of Hebraic origin, argued the Greek-speaking believers, were getting favored treatment.[2]

The church leaders recognized that the issue was deeper than food distribution. The unity of the church was at stake. The matter threatened to be a major distraction to the young congregation. The leaders could have succumbed to the tyranny of the urgent and taken care of the situation themselves. Instead, they appointed seven well-respected people to deal with the ministry issue and address the festering division.

The reason they gave for not stepping in themselves was the need to maintain their focus on the proper priorities: "Then we apostles can spend our time in prayer and teaching the word."[3]

Did you catch that? The leaders of the first church had

two priorities: teaching the Word of God and concentrating on prayer.

The focus of the apostles kept the church moving forward evangelistically: "So God's message continued to spread. The number of believers greatly increased in Jerusalem, and many of the Jewish priests were converted, too."[4]

Why Our Churches Are Praying More

There is no doubt that times of crisis prompt church members to pray more often and more fervently. There is also little doubt that the pandemic was a crisis prompting much prayer.

People prayed for friends and loved ones who were stricken by COVID-19. They prayed for economic issues as millions lost their jobs. They prayed for those who were lonely, depressed, and seeking answers for the pain around them.

It seemed, however, that the impetus behind this prayer movement was broader than the immediate crisis at hand. For many church members, it was a time of discovering their purpose. Although they had been involved in a church for years, their efforts were largely activity driven or done out of a sense of duty.

"I think I was going through the motions at my church for the most part," a woman named Maureen told us. She had been at her church for more than thirty years. "The coronavirus kept me stuck at home for a long time and gave me a lot of time to think and pray. I am in a large community group at my church. We began praying for our church and sharing prayer needs with each other."

She paused to gather her thoughts. "What we started doing in our community group grew naturally to other parts of the church. We eventually formed a Facebook group. It really began to grow at that point."

Maureen's voice grew more intense. "The Facebook group was the vehicle to get us praying for our community. It was pretty basic. When people saw we were praying, they asked us to pray for them. We prayed for a lot of people with physical problems and sicknesses. Some of them had the coronavirus. We were blessed because nobody we prayed for died.

"Somehow, the mayor found out about our prayer ministry," Maureen continued. "She has been mayor for seven years, and most people in the town really like her. When she came to our Facebook page, requesting prayer for different needs in the community, the response was awesome. It was like our church became the prayer arm of the town. More and more people joined our Facebook page and either requested prayer or prayed for others."

Maureen paused again and became more reflective. "You know," she said, "for most of my life, I viewed church as a bunch of religious activities. I went to church more out of obligation than anything else. Now I realize more and more I *am* the church, at least part of it."

Her smile was natural and contagious. "I will never look at church the same way again," she concluded. "I have never really thought I could make much of a difference, but now I know I can. And to think it took a pandemic and a quarantine to wake me up from my spiritual slumber."

She closed our conversation with emphasis. "I will never view church the same way again."

New Roman Roads for the Church

With all the focus on digital technology in our day, it's easy to overlook how God used the cutting-edge technology of earlier ages to spread the gospel across the globe. One such technology was the Romans' expertise in building roads. Beginning in 312 BC with the Appian Way, the Romans kicked off a major construction project that ultimately included 50,000 miles of roadway.

These roads were technological marvels. Some were small, local roads; others were like interstate highways connecting major cities and military bases. They were often exceptionally durable, including stone-paved roadways that lasted for centuries, down to the modern era. The roadbeds usually were cambered for drainage and flanked by footpaths. The Roman roads cut through hills and traversed rivers and ravines on bridges. Large sections of roads went through marshy grounds atop rafted or piled foundations.[5]

Though the Romans' intent was to facilitate the growth of the empire, the most important, albeit unintended, consequence was the propulsion of the Christian gospel throughout southern Europe and Asia Minor.

During the COVID-19 pandemic, the roadways of digital technology became a major conduit for prayer ministries to travel. Groups would gather online for Zoom-enabled prayer meetings. Social media became a vehicle for prayer requests and testimonies of prayers answered. Smartphones were ubiquitous tools at the ready to transform a prayer ministry instantaneously.

Some would argue that digital technology is an instrument of evil. Opinion is certainly divided on the subject.[6] There is no question technology can be used in innumerable dark and tragic ways. One does not have to spend much time on social media to sense a pervasive presence of darkness and negativity.

But technology can also be used for good. It is indeed the modern Roman road to carry the gospel to unreached persons and places.

The Roman road of the first century was used for wartime activity. It was a hideout for thieves and murderers. It was a conduit for all types of nefarious trafficking.

Those same Roman roads were pathways that early followers of Jesus took to share the good news of the Savior's resurrection. If you trace the land paths of the apostle Paul's missionary journeys, you will see much of it carrying forward on Roman roads.

Like any instrument, digital technology can be used for evil. But God uses it for good.

The quarantine was not just a time when many church leaders discovered how to stream worship services online. It was also a time when a multiplicity of new ministries exploded. People who had never before heard the church's name were reached. And as we've mentioned, prayer ministries were foremost among the emerging ministries with unparalleled impact in the digital world. For certain, as churches regather and attempt to return to a semblance of rhythm, there is bound to be a diminishing of the intensive impact of some of these ministries. The intensity and fervor will wane. But churches will not abandon the instruments they used in the quarantine era as they settle into the post-quarantine age. There is no turning back.

The post-quarantine church is moving into a time of pervasive and powerful prayer. To miss this opportunity is to miss a clear movement of God.

Practical Examples of Prayer Ministries

The principle of ebb and flow is always present in church ministry, and prayer ministries are no exception. Stated simply, there will be times of increased fervor for corporate prayer and times when it will decline. As the quarantine eased, we saw a heightened interest in and commitment to prayer. In the days ahead, as the initial enthusiasm gives way to the need for a sustainable, long-term commitment, it will be important for churches to plan for more structured ways to encourage people to pray.

So how do churches create a framework for prayer?

Some churches have a room set aside for people to pray. Unfortunately, prayer rooms are often unused rooms. I consulted with one church that used the prayer room for storage. The message about the church's low priority of prayer was painfully evident.

A church in Arkansas probably focused on prayer better than any congregation I've seen. For a decade, they had someone praying twenty-four hours a day every day of the week. As each person finished praying, he or she was responsible for calling the next person in line. So the church member who prayed from 2:00 a.m. to 3:00 a.m. on Thursdays called the person responsible for praying next at 3:00 a.m.

A prayer ministry we founded at Church Answers is being used in many churches around the world. The ministry, called Pray and Go (prayandgochurch.com), seeks to combine the mandates of the Great Commission and Christ's mandate for all believers to pray.

The concept is simple. Church members go into the community and pray for homes they walk by. After the members pray, they leave a hanger on the door to let the residents know someone prayed for them. Residents have the opportunity to connect with the church or make prayer requests. The ministry can be done by almost anyone in the church.

The keys to a successful prayer ministry are threefold. First, church leadership must be intentional about keeping prayer at the forefront of the congregation's priorities. As churches have moved from quarantine to post-quarantine, there has still been a strong emphasis on prayer. That momentum was given by God to the church in a challenging season. It must be continued and cultivated.

Second, church leaders should promote periodic prayer emphases to restoke the fire. Remember the principle of ebb and flow. Churches cannot indefinitely maintain initiatives that require a lot of intensity. Unfortunately, most church leaders move on to the tyranny of the urgent when a prayer enterprise begins to subside. Instead, they should be planning for the next season of emphasis. It could be a year away, but the members must be encouraged to make corporate prayer a regular priority.

Keep in mind the story of the first church in Jerusalem. The congregation was at great risk of losing their focus on prayer and the Great Commission. The argument between those who supported the Greek widows and those who supported the Hebrew widows had become a major distraction. The situation was described as "rumblings of discontent."[7]

Remember their solutions as well. For sure, the widows needed the ministry. The leaders of the church took care of that matter by equipping others to do the work of ministry.[8]

While making provision for other ministry to flourish, the apostles made certain to keep their focus on two things: prayer and the teaching of the Word. This emphasis kept the church focused where they needed to be. As a consequence "the number of believers greatly increased."[9]

Third, members should be encouraged to *pray* and *wait*. There will not always be immediate and apparent answers.

Just look at the examples of Abraham and Sarah as they waited for their promised son. Members must be reminded from time to time of God's invisible hand at work. Don't lose the emphasis. Don't stop praying.

What Will Be the Markers of the COVID-19 Quarantine?

With rare exception, the markers of history are not known at the moment they occur. Unless an event is a major milestone or tragedy, we often don't see how history is shaping around us.

The pandemic is a case in point, particularly for churches. We can only speculate how God is working to shape the post-quarantine era. But we can see some early indicators, both good and bad. From a negative perspective, we see more churches closing. Most of these churches were already in decline; the pandemic simply accelerated their demise. To use the metaphor of COVID-19, their deaths were the result of a new disease combined with underlying conditions.

On the plus side, we also know that many churches entered the post-quarantine era with greater determination and—more important—greater dependence on God. Many of these churches will be stronger and more effective. Many of them will help other churches become more effective as well.

In the early days of the quarantine, a number of church leaders and members worried that their finances would drop significantly and they would have insufficient funds to support and continue ministries. While that scenario proved true for some churches, it was certainly not the case for many others. To the contrary, many congregations became financially stronger.

Another telling indicator that will likely emerge in the post-quarantine era is the way many churches adapted and innovated. This creative spirit was evident during the quarantine in churches of all sizes and locations. These congregations did not merely demonstrate their resilience; they demonstrated a newfound strength to march forward. Many are already reaping the benefits in the post-quarantine days.

One of the points of progress I will be monitoring most closely is that of increased prayer intensity. Certainly we saw prayer become a primary focus during the pandemic. Will that intensity carry forward in the months and years ahead?

Even more, will we look back on the pandemic as the beginning of a new spiritual awakening across the globe? Was the movement of prayer used by God to bring a true revival to our land? Only time will tell.

But this one thing we can know for certain: God honors praying churches. He answers the prayers of praying people. Though we can only wait and see if a powerful spiritual awakening will follow, in the meantime we can do everything through God's power to make certain our churches are praying churches.

We saw prayer taken to a new and powerful level during the quarantine. If we are obedient and continue to be houses of prayer—if a perpetual posture of prayer truly takes root in our churches—we might say the pandemic was used by God in a powerful way like few events we have known.

Three Thoughts

1. Think about the prayer ministries that took place in your church during the pandemic. Think about whether they are still present today.

2. Think about other church members who may join you in praying for your church and community on a regular basis.

3. Think about the technologies your church used during the pandemic and the ways those technologies can be used for prayer ministries today.

RETHINK YOUR FACILITIES FOR EMERGING OPPORTUNITIES

My team and I have been consulting with churches for more than thirty years.

You can arrive at two conclusions from that statement. First, we have a lot of experience. Second, I'm old.

You would be right on both counts.

We have done hundreds of on-site consultations and thousands of telephone consultations. In recent years, we have added video consultations.

Though every congregation is different, many have a number of similarities. In fact, we see patterns that become surprisingly predictable. One pastor surmised that I had already made conclusions about his church after the first day of our on-site consultation. His statement wasn't completely accurate, but a few of my early predications did prove true.

There are many common patterns among churches.

One particular and fairly recent consultation comes to mind. I began describing this church in the first chapter. Allow me to expand on the story.

The church in question had been slowly declining for eight consecutive years. Though the decline was never dramatic in any one year, the cumulative effect over multiple years was discouraging to the church leaders and membership.

After five years of decreasing attendance, the leaders became convinced that the problem lay in their dated and inadequate facilities. To be clear, the church had plenty of space for both worship attenders and small-group on-campus attenders. They just felt that the facilities did not offer a draw to the surrounding community.

So the church embarked on a multimillion-dollar renovation and construction project. They were fortunate that the church members generously gave to the campaign, so the church did not incur much debt.

The worship center was renovated. The fellowship hall and kitchen got a total makeover. Offices and classrooms were updated. And the centerpiece of the project was a newly constructed activities building, including a gym and flexible space for large and small gatherings.

The project was completed. Celebratory services ensued. And the church leaders and members waited for more people to show up.

The decline continued unabated.

The church leadership was bewildered, frustrated, and

embarrassed. They had been so certain that new and updated facilities would be the solution to years of decline. Eventually, they called in our team at Church Answers.

Because the renovated buildings were such a key piece of their growth strategy, I decided to join two of my team members on a tour of the facilities. An elder of the church graciously and proudly showed us around.

The work was indeed impressive. Everything looked welcoming and updated. The activities building was stunning and highly functional.

As we entered this new building, I noticed a rather thick publication on a desk. I could not help but see its title: "Policies and Procedures for the Use of Church Facilities." I asked the elder if I could look at it. He welcomed me to do so.

I was stunned. I felt as if I were reading a government document. The restrictions and regulations for using the building were voluminous. I couldn't even remember all the rules after I was done. But one particular stipulation stuck out to me. To the best of my recollection, it read something like this: "Nonmembers of the church are not allowed to use the building unless they are guests of a member. Church members must accompany nonmembers at all times."

Ugh.

I asked the elder why these restrictions and policies were in place, and I could have anticipated his response. He told us that people from the community who started coming to the building were "really messing the place up." Instead of having a few simple guidelines for everyone to follow, the church decided to make sure that community members were not allowed in the building on their own. Before long, non-members stopped using the building.

A New Mindset on Church Facilities

The church we visited had a bigger issue than creating a figurative moat around their facilities. The overarching problem was their mindset. They were inwardly focused. The church had become an exclusive social club, and membership had its privileges. The programs, ministries, resources, and facilities were essentially for insiders only. The Great Commission had become a great *omission*.

Not all of our consultations lead to the results or responses we desire. This one, however, had a surprisingly positive conclusion. The leadership took to heart our assessment that the church either had to develop a new mindset or it would continue on the path of decline. The pastor made a bold statement that would prove pivotal in their new path: "We have become a pseudo-spiritual country club."

As we followed up with the church leaders after the on-site consultation, we worked with them through the challenges they inevitably encountered. Specifically, most of the members had grown comfortable with the country club mindset of the church. They liked having their own preferences met. They truly wanted the church their way and no other way.

Though the obstacles were ever present, the leadership persisted, and the church gradually became more outwardly focused. Some of the earliest efforts were focused on establishing a new mindset about their facilities. Those changes particularly irked the subset of members who viewed the new activities building as an exclusive domain for their own use.

In many ways, the pastor shared with me on a video call, opening the facilities to the community was the impetus that moved the church forward. After all, the buildings, and particularly the activities center, were the most visible symbols of an inward focus. When the leadership began making changes in how the buildings would be used, other moves that fostered an outward focus quickly followed.

We often hear that "the building is not the church; the people are." Most often, that sentiment is articulated when we talk about church attendance or church facilities. In either case, the conversation is about church members and community members coming to a physical location where the church gathers.

I am unapologetic about advocating faithful attendance. The church gathered, whether it's in a building, in a home, or out in a field, is a vital part of church life. I don't even hesitate to use the phrase that often gets the most resistance: "I am going to church." I guess I need to be more theologically precise and say that I am going to *gather with* the church.

Similarly, I can see much good that comes from the right use of church facilities. For certain, too many churches are poor stewards of their buildings. Their occupancy rate is as bad as a college football stadium. Weekdays are usually devoid of people in most church facilities.

But that doesn't have to be the fate of a church building. Instead of arguing semantics about "going to church," many church leaders are beginning to see that their facilities can be a powerfully useful tool for ministry. But that can only happen with a change in mindset.

As I noted in the first chapter, church leaders and members recognized during the quarantine that the church still existed—beyond its physical facilities. Aided by the relatively new tools of digital technology, church members were able to worship together, albeit remotely. They were able to pray together, to study the Bible together, and to minister to others together.

Paradoxically, while these leaders and members were learning that the church could remain effective without buildings during the pandemic, they also began to miss the facilities they were not allowed to enter. Buildings were not required; but buildings could be useful and desirable tools for ministry.

The pandemic brought a shift in mindset about church facilities. Though they were not absolutely required for ministry to occur, they were nonetheless God's gifts of resources that could be used for his glory.

The post-quarantine church, then, has a vibrant opportunity to rethink how we use our facilities. Even at this point in the regathering and reopening, we are seeing definitive moves in this direction.

Facilities for the Community

I recently led a fun exercise with several church leaders. All of the pastors were given a demographic and psychographic report of their respective communities. Their communities were defined by the typical amount of time most church attenders take to drive to a worship service. The most common drive time was ten minutes.

We used a helpful tool we provide at Church Answers called the Know Your Community report (you can find it at churchanswers.com/solutions/tools/know-your-community/). The assignment was simple: Look at the demographics and psychographics of your community to discover five ways your church facilities can be used to *reach* your community. We reminded the pastors that demographics define the statistical characteristics of populations, such as age, income, gender, race, and other factors. Psychographics define the population according to their attitudes, aspirations, and behaviors.

The pastors took an hour to pore over the data in their respective reports. You could sense the energy in the room as they began to open their minds to new possibilities.

When we reconvened, I explained that the simple purpose of the exercise was to help them develop a different mindset about their church facilities. The key is to see the church building from the perspective of the *community* rather than their church members. To be clear, the church buildings are still meant to be used by church members as well, but most churches do not consider the community's perspective.

I was greatly encouraged by their responses.

Marvin, a pastor from Oklahoma, knew the neighborhoods near his church had a lot of young families. But he was shocked to discover that the number of children under twelve years old was twice the national average. He had never led his congregation to be intentional about reaching these young families.

"We have two things going for us," Marvin shared with enthusiasm. "We have a great children's minister. She loves her ministry and she loves the kids."

Marvin continued, "We also have a Parents' Night Out forty weeks out of the year. Our younger parents in the church really take advantage of this ministry."

He smiled and said with excitement, "But we have never done anything to extend these ministries to families in the community without a church home. It's always been a ministry and service for the members of the church. It wouldn't take much at all to get the word out. We don't have to reinvent the wheel. We just need to convert these two ministries from a members-only mindset to a community outreach."

Andrew, a pastor from a church near Sacramento, had an especially poignant story to tell. As I watched him surveying the demographics for his area, I saw tears falling from his eyes. I asked him if he was okay.

"Look at this line," he showed me with a trembling hand. "Look at the number of single moms within a twelve-minute drive of our church. Imagine all the struggles they face."

Andrew paused and took a deep breath. "I've been at

my church for about five years, and in all that time, we have done nothing, *zero*, to minister to these single moms. Our mission field is right under our noses, and I totally missed it."

He began to name several possible ministries to reach these moms. "My guess is that childcare is a huge need. We don't have a daycare or a preschool, but we could offer a Parents' Night Out like Marvin described in his church. We could offer after-school care. The possibilities are endless. I guess we need to start asking these moms how we can best serve them."

The demographics of Rick's church in Florida skewed older, which made sense because one of the state's larger retirement communities was within ten minutes of his church. "I'm not surprised by these numbers," Rick said. "But I have never considered them through the lens of reaching the older Boomers with our facilities. Now my mind is churning with ideas. If our area is dominated by older adults, we should use our facilities to reach them."

These are the types of conversations that began in great number during the pandemic. Now, in the post-quarantine world, the question is being asked again in earnest: How can we use our facilities to reach and minister to our community?

It's a good question.

Partnerships with the Community

As the world emerges more completely from the quarantine and more activities resume, watch for an increasing number of facilities partnerships between churches and community organizations. A number of African American congregations have been on the cutting edge of this movement for many years, but most churches have avoided these relationships for a number of reasons.[1]

The most common reason is a lack of knowledge or experience. It simply hasn't been the practice of most North American congregations to share their facilities with outside groups. In other words, "We've never done it that way before."

Our team often hears church leaders say that such partnerships can't be done, particularly between a not-for-profit church and a for-profit business. The common fear is loss of their nonprofit status. Though, certainly, church leaders should seek legal and financial guidance before initiating a partnership, it simply isn't true they can't be done. In fact, many churches have been sharing their facilities legally and ethically for years.

Partnerships with governmental entities are also possible. As I noted earlier, I was recently in a church where significant space was used by the local police as a substation. Churches have been using public school space for years, particularly for church plants. Look for the trend to reciprocate, with schools making use of church space.

Historically, most church leaders have been comfortable sharing space with other nonprofit organizations, particularly if they have a complementary mission. Expect these types of relationships to increase in the months and years ahead.

The plain truth is that most churches have been woefully inefficient in the use of their facilities. Let's call it what it is: poor stewardship. Year in and year out, hundreds of millions of dollars of land and buildings have sat idle for most of the week. Fortunately, this long-term practice is finally changing. There were signs of change even before the pandemic, but now that pastors, staff, and congregants have survived an extended period with no facilities, they have become more acutely aware of the need for—and potential benefits of—change. An average 10 percent occupancy rate simply cannot continue.

"If we were able to be the church without buildings," a Wisconsin pastor shared with us, "there is absolutely no reason why we can't use our buildings more effectively. We have to see them as tools for ministry." One obvious way to utilize these tools is by making church facilities available for other organizations to use.

This trend may be partially motivated by the desire to share the cost of expensive and often aging buildings. But the motivation must extend beyond financial stewardship. Church leaders must begin to realize that a facility partnership with a local organization is an avenue for the church to truly reach its neighbors.

When the church opens its doors to the community by making its buildings available for other uses, the community "comes to church." Such partnerships have gospel opportunities written all over them.

The Post-Quarantine Worship Center

In the first chapter, I began a discussion about the physical worship center or sanctuary. Let's expand on those thoughts.

For half a century, the size of the sanctuary or worship center was often seen as an indicator of church success and health. Led typically by pastors from the Builder (born before 1946) and Boomer (born 1946–1964) generations, these congregations often seemed to be in a race to construct the latest and largest building.

Read the history of many churches in the last fifty years on the church's website. Their historical markers were often new construction, renovated facilities, or relocation to larger sites. If someone who knew nothing about the church read these histories, he or she would likely conclude that the most successful churches were those with the biggest and newest facilities.

Many large churches built facilities capable of seating thousands in a single service. These churches were often touted as among the best in the world.

Then the tide shifted.

Some of the changes were part of a cultural religious shift. As the general population became more secular, people were less likely to attend church worship services. Some of the changes were due to the weakening commitments of church members. Those who once attended four times a month were now showing up only twice a month. And some of the changes were preferential. Anecdotal evidence suggests that

Gen X, Millennials, and Gen Z prefer nonconventional worship gatherings. Indeed, it seems likely that only the Boomer generation preferred the "big box" services.

A number of larger churches adjusted to the shift toward smaller venues by becoming multisite and multivenue. Indeed, it is rare to see a large, growing church that is not multisite today. Many smaller churches have also become multisite.

Then the pandemic hit, and churches of all shapes and sizes could no longer meet in their buildings. Most of them did well transitioning to digital streaming services, but the quarantine also gave church leaders time—and a reason—to rethink how they used their facilities for worship services. A number of leaders realized that "the usual way" of conducting worship services was for a bygone era. Two or three hours on Sunday morning worked well in an agrarian society, but those days are long behind us now. Most churches today are not populated by a lot of farmers.

Church leaders also began to realize they would have to be creative as they returned to in-person services. The ratio of congregants to available space and the need for social distancing (at least initially) meant these leaders had to rethink their worship services.

What transpired in many churches was a rethinking of how the sanctuary or worship center would be used in the post-quarantine era. In the early stages of regathering, the most common adjustment—and perhaps the least creative—was adding to the number of services. Of course, every leader knows that any kind of change in an organization engenders pain, even if the change is not highly innovative.

Two other early changes were obvious. First, more churches decided they could have worship services at times other than Sunday morning. They finally began to respond to the demographic reality that as many as one-third of working adults have to work on Sunday mornings.[2]

Second, the online services that either began or were augmented during the quarantine are not going away. Regarding digital and in-person services, church leaders will continue to wrestle with the challenges of both/and instead of either/or.

Perhaps the most basic and obvious conclusion to be drawn from the pandemic is that it gave church leaders an opportunity to rethink *everything*, including the use of their physical facilities. It is an opportunity I call "the blank slate."

But if church leaders and members don't take this opportunity to rethink everything they've been doing, it will indeed be an opportunity wasted. God may be waiting for you to write a new story for your church on the blank slate he has provided.

Three Thoughts

1. Think about how your church facilities were used before the pandemic and how that is changing and might change more.

2. Think of ways that your church may partner with another organization in the use of your church facilities.

3. Think about how the digital streaming of services during the pandemic might change the future of your worship services in your physical facilities.

MAKE LASTING CHANGES THAT WILL MAKE A DIFFERENCE

Your church has entered a new era.

To be clear, your church was already moving in that direction, but the pace has been greatly accelerated by the pandemic. Where you are today, in terms of rethinking and retooling your ministries, probably would have taken another five years without the coronavirus. But those changes were coming. That's an important truth to understand and embrace.

The pace of change due to the pandemic has been dramatic for many churches. Many leaders are uncertain how to lead in this new environment. Many church members are confused and fearful. Where do you go from here?

At this point, no one can know precisely what lies ahead. In fact, it could be a few years before we arrive at any semblance of a new normal. You are navigating uncharted waters, and every day will bring new challenges. To lead successfully, you will have to pivot. To lead successfully, you will need to make some changes on the fly.

This may be the last thing you want to hear, but to lead successfully in the post-quarantine church, you will have to lead without total clarity. You will have to lead with a lot of uncertainty.

If anything has become clear, it's this: You can no longer lead according to bygone expectations, perspectives, and methodologies. A new era requires a new approach if you want to successfully reach the people God has placed in your path.

But before we take a closer look at the need for change, let's take a step back and remind ourselves of two things that never change: God's wisdom and his faithfulness. You know he has this situation in hand, even if you're not at all sure what he has in store.

If you find yourself wavering at this point—or even if you're fully on board and ready to roll—allow me to point you back to how the apostles responded to a time of tremendous change in the earliest days of the church: They devoted themselves to prayer and the Word of God.[1] Whatever else may come, *prayer* and *God's Word* must be front-and-center priorities for the path ahead.

In the coming seasons of uncertainty, you will be required to lead change, perhaps like you never have before. You will make decisions one day, embrace some of them the next day, and discard others the day after that.

I have attempted to lead you through some of the challenges you will likely face, but it's far too early to have a full grasp of what lies ahead. So in this chapter, let's discuss the issue of change itself. We've looked at issues that will likely change, so let's look now at how we might best lead in the midst of those changes.

Failures to Avoid in Leading Change

Let's start by reviewing some key issues for leading change. Whether you're a pastor, staff member, lay leader, or other active member, you must be ready to deal with significant changes in your church. Though we are approaching it from a negative perspective—avoiding failure—it's worth noting that the obstacles to change have been around for decades. If these warnings were needed *before* the pandemic, they are needed more than ever in the post-quarantine era.

Lack of urgency. During the quarantine, church members likely embraced the need to respond urgently. After all, they had to adapt almost overnight to the shift from in-person worship services to online meetings. Many also had to embrace a new format for their small groups. A lot of church members learned the intricacies of video conferencing in a matter of hours. The need for urgency was obvious; and for the most part, urgency was embraced.

Now, a percentage of church members are waiting for church to return to the old normal. It won't. And because we may not know for even a few years what the new normal will look like, church leaders must continue to lead with urgency. They must help their members understand that we are on a new mission field, and we will be exploring and discovering this new land for the foreseeable future.

Bottom line: We can't do things the way we've always done them.

Failure to gain influential allies. No church leader can lead this rapid change alone. All must seek the help of influential people in the church who can work with other church members to embrace the need and the means for change. Without these allies, leaders will be blazing a trail with no followers. That's not leadership.

No clear vision. The concept of vision is changing rapidly in churches, particularly in regard to time frame. Church leaders have been accustomed to communicating a vision that covers three, five, or even ten years. No more. In the post-quarantine era, vision casting will be measured in months. Simply stated, we can't see much beyond a year at this point.

So what does that mean for those who want to lead with as clear a vision as possible? It will mean enhancing your ability to lead through short-term projects and casting a clear and compelling vision for those short-term ideas. In other words, if you fail to create short-term wins, you will struggle to lead effective change. Let's briefly look at that issue more closely.

Failure to create short-term wins. Your church is moving into an era of significant disruption and uncertainty. It is unlikely that anyone can see beyond a few months at a time. Leaders, your members will need encouragement now more than ever. What can you lead your church to accomplish over the next four to twelve months? What successes can you celebrate sooner rather than later? These celebrations will be vitally important for your church to move forward against the headwinds of uncertainty.

Failure to communicate a thousand times more. Okay, maybe "a thousand times more" is a bit of hyperbole. Or maybe not. Most leaders think their followers grasp a message the first or second time they hear it. In reality, it takes multiple iterations of communication over an extended period of time for something to be understood, let alone embraced, by followers.

Do you remember how often governmental leaders around the world communicated during the pandemic? Some had daily briefings. In times of uncertainty, leaders must increase the frequency of communication. Be prepared as church leaders to become frequent communicators during the days of post-quarantine uncertainty.

Giving obstacles too much attention. I know it sounds terrible to refer to some church members as obstacles. But some people are just that. They are negative naysayers. If you let them hold the church back during this time of turbulent change, your congregation will not make the transformative changes necessary to thrive in the post-pandemic world.

Love your naysayers. Pray for your naysayers. With discernment, listen to your naysayers. But don't allow them to undermine the momentum of a congregation that is ready and willing to move forward.

So how do we successfully lead change in these uncertain days? Most effective change leaders will follow seven key principles.

Seven Ways to Lead for Lasting Change

For years, we have worked with and observed leaders who are effective in leading change in the church. The key is not only to lead change but to lead change that will last.

Many church leaders commented on how receptive to change their church members became during the pandemic. That's not surprising. The need for change is more easily embraced during times of crisis. But most church members will be expecting a return to the old normal. So let's say it again: Those days are gone forever. Leaders must lead in a new and unsettling time. Here are seven principles that the most effective leaders of lasting change have followed.

1. Remind People of Their Biblical Hope

The Bible contains one story after another about change. Abraham led his family to an unknown land. Moses led the people of Israel out of Egypt toward a new land of promise. Joshua led the people into both the promises and challenges of the new land. The early followers of Jesus traveled on missionary journeys from one town to another, often at great cost and great risk.

Why were they willing to make such great sacrifices? They trusted God. They believed God had a better plan for them. They had hope because God gave them hope.

Here's something important we need to understand: The relatively stable times that churches in North America have enjoyed over the past two centuries are an aberration—certainly compared to other parts of the world and down through the history of the church. An argument could also be made that comfort and stability are unhealthy for the church. When the writer of Hebrews describes the heroes of the faith in Hebrews 11, he uses terms that speak of discomfort rather than comfort.

For example, Abraham, Isaac, and Jacob are described as foreigners every place they traveled. They were not expected or allowed to become comfortable.

> It was by faith that Abraham obeyed when God called him to leave home and go to another land that God would give him as his inheritance. He went without knowing where he was going. And even when he reached the land God promised him, he lived there by faith—for he was like a foreigner, living in tents. And so did Isaac and Jacob, who inherited the same promise. Abraham was confidently looking forward to a city with eternal foundations, a city designed and built by God.[2]

I followed the words of encouragement and hope offered by many pastors as they led their churches into the post-quarantine era. And it was encouraging to see the majority of them preparing their congregations well.

Here is one example of how a pastor communicated words of hope to his congregation: "We pivoted constantly. We weren't afraid to try things we'd never done before. New information each week meant we had to try new things all the time."

He also addressed the opportunities made possible by digital technology: "Church online will never be an afterthought to our church again. It is a part of our new reality."

And this pastor was transparent about his own uncertainty while communicating a clear message of hope: "I admit I am a bit nervous for our church as we enter a new season," he wrote. "But I am proud of our church. You understood we were not doing this alone. And you understood we would go into this new season with great hope because the Spirit will guide us and strengthen us every step of the way."

2. Remember, Cultural Change Comes Last

A number of leaders have attempted to change the culture as a first step toward lasting change. It always fails. We cannot declare through sermons and other forms of communication that the membership must shift their cultural reality. Cultural shifts are the ends, not the means.

It reminds me of a leadership meeting I attended many

years ago in an organization whose culture was characterized by fear and confusion. As the leader commenced the meeting, he demanded, "I want all of you to get happy!" It did not go over well.

We cannot demand or declare a new and healthy culture into existence. Culture is the result of cumulative actions, not something we do to fix attitudes and environments. Allow me to give an example in the context of marriage.

Nellie Jo and I have been married a long time. In fact, we have been dating or married three-fourths of our lives. Our marriage is healthy but not perfect. One of the better transformational times in our marriage began when I asked Nellie Jo if we could take the Love Dare challenge.

The Love Dare is a book for husbands and wives to walk through together for forty days.[3] Each daily reading ends with a "dare": a positive action by each spouse on behalf of the other. By the end of forty days, the husband and wife will have taken forty specific actions to encourage each other and strengthen their marriage.

I can attest that the culture of our marriage was transformed by specific and positive actions. I didn't declare at the outset that Nellie Jo and I needed to be happier in our marriage. Our marriage became happier and healthier as a result of what we did during the forty days.

Your church culture will change in the right direction if you consistently lead your congregation with specific and positive steps. Most likely, you don't yet know what those steps will be. But they will become evident as you begin to address the challenges and opportunities in your church. God will make them clear.

Always have an attitude of action. If not, your church will miss opportunities that arise in the post-quarantine era.

3. Visible Action Steps Are Essential

I have written a lot of books with *church* in the title. But one book I *haven't* written might describe the state of most congregations, particularly American congregations: *Routine Church.*

Our churches have been slow to change. Worship times are the same as ever. Order of worship is often the same year in, year out. Programs and ministries ebb and flow but stay roughly the same overall.

This pattern is not limited to older, more established churches. Even newer churches get caught up in the busyness of church life and fail to take innovative action steps on a regular basis.

We have been feeling that internal tug for years in our churches. The surrounding culture is shifting. Growth and health are more challenging to maintain. We can't continue to "do church" the way we've always done it and expect Great Commission results.

When the pandemic hit, this difficult situation was exacerbated by something we did not see coming. Reaching people had been challenging before social distancing; now it became *painfully* challenging.

A social media post connected to an article I wrote paints a vivid picture of just one of the challenges churches are facing in the post-quarantine era. The writer identified herself as Susan, a person who had been active in her church for many years.

> I have been going to church for so many years I
> don't even know how long it's been. It was what
> I was supposed to do. Now I sleep in on Sunday,
> and I may or may not watch the Facebook service.
> I really like this new schedule. I am really not sure
> I want to go back to church like I used to. It's a big
> hassle.

In the post-quarantine era, what will compel the Susans of the world to return to in-person gatherings? Among other factors, they will need to see a church that is making a difference, a church that is truly touching lives. And they will need to see consistent *action* directed outward toward the community. It is no longer sufficient for a church to have a cleverly worded vision statement. They must back up the words with action.

The need for an outward focus and corresponding action is the same as it was before the pandemic. But now the need is exponentially more urgent. Churches must demonstrate short-term wins and ongoing movement in the community and for the community. Yesterday's long-term planning teams must become today's short-term action groups.

4. Allies Are Still Imperative

As we noted earlier, a common pitfall for pastors who lead change is the failure to cultivate allies. This issue is now imperative for post-quarantine changes.

During the pandemic, we noticed a number of leaders working with influencers in the church to prepare the congregation for change. The most effective leaders were not only focused on leading change during the pandemic; they were also developing allies for the future, when churches could gather again.

Now, as churches regather in the post-quarantine era—both digitally and in-person—these alliances have taken on even greater importance. The key influencers have the ears of the congregation, who look to them for both formal and informal authority. Church members not only want to hear from their pastors, elders, staff, and other positional leaders, they want to hear from these informal leaders, whom they trust and follow.

In the post-quarantine church, change will happen more rapidly than most church members have ever seen. Culture was shifting decisively before the pandemic. It is now shifting at a breathtaking pace. Church members must hear from their leaders that God is in control and that the church is moving forward in his strength. But they must also hear these positive, reassuring messages from those who are not in formal leadership positions.

Collaboration is imperative. Develop allies of influence, regardless of their roles in the church.

5. Communication Must Increase Exponentially

Yes, communication is vital in any period of change—which is to say, *always*. But the church is entering a new era, a time that can be both confusing and intimidating. There is greater uncertainty now about the future of local congregations than I can recall in my lifetime.

Every church needs to update its approach. Every church needs assurance that the changes underway are for the better. Every church needs to know the direction they are headed.

Communication must come from the pulpit. From the church's website. From social media. From newsletters. From informal conversations. From meetings.

Repeat.

And repeat again.

Simply stated, there is no such thing as overcommunication in changing times. Good communication is one of the primary traits needed in effective leaders. This trait will be invaluable in the post-quarantine church.

6. Leaders Must Be Willing to Accept Membership Losses

This challenge will be among the greatest for leaders of churches in this era. No pastor or church leader likes to lose members. It is typically painful for pastors to lose even the most negative of church members. When members leave the church, it is often an issue of concern among other church members. It becomes an issue of morale and unity.

Change is difficult enough in churches. But the pace of

change necessary for the post-quarantine era will be rapid. Some members will not be able to keep up. Others will become frustrated. Some will become angry to the point of leaving.

Church leaders will rightly desire to be pastoral to these hurting church members. Indeed, those who struggle with change will need and deserve prayerful attention. However, we want to be certain not to give so much attention to negative members that the healthy church members are neglected. Likewise, we don't want to expend so much energy on the detractors that the church loses its focus.

Indeed, the mission of the church can be compromised and undermined when the naysayers get inordinate attention. Church leaders, sadly, must be willing to let go of some church members. The post-quarantine era can either be a time of great opportunity or a time of great struggle. One of the key issues will be dealing with the reality of membership losses.

7. Leaders Must Align with the Future

Simply stated, church leaders must consider every decision based on the new realities of the post-quarantine world. That's what it means to align with the future.

For example, when staff members leave, consider how to replace (or not replace) them with the needs of the emerging new culture in mind.

If your church has been busy maintaining a lot of

programs, consider whether some need to be eliminated or moved to a digital platform.

As your church makes decisions about facilities, consider the new realities of the gathered and scattered church.

If your church decides to increase the emphasis on small groups, consider whether there are new and better ways for people to gather.

In other words, the rules have changed in the post-quarantine era. Get ready to adapt.

One church leader handled a personnel issue with foresight and creativity. When the associate pastor retired during the pandemic, the lead pastor looked toward the future. Instead of replacing the retiring pastor with another associate pastor with the same job description, the church decided to add a teaching pastor whose primary responsibilities would be the church's digital ministries. As of this writing, the church has three good candidates. Not surprisingly, all three are relatively young and already proficient in digital technologies. By rethinking the needs of their church and their community, the leaders are able to pivot to a new ministry approach.

The essence of leading for change is leading for *lasting* change. As churches continue to adapt in the post-quarantine era, many church members will likely expect things to return to the old normal. But that can't happen if the church is to survive, and thrive, in the post-pandemic era. Leaders must lead with the new realities in view.

Three Thoughts

1. Think about how receptive to change your church was during the quarantine, and note the lessons you can learn from that period.

2. Think about where some of the most beneficial change has already taken place in your church.

3. Think about where your church may face some of its greatest challenges in adapting and changing in the post-quarantine era.

FROM CHALLENGES TO OPPORTUNITIES

It's easier to speak with certainty and clarity about what is *not* changing in the post-quarantine church.

The Bible is still the Word of God.

Christ is still the only way of salvation.

Prayer is still vital.

Evangelism is still a mandate.

No doubt we could expand the list.

The God we serve is the same yesterday, today, and forever. But for leaders and church members in the post-quarantine era, change is coming at an accelerated pace. I think by now you've probably gotten that message pretty clearly. Churches that refuse to change will inevitably decline or even die. Blunt but true.

In the previous chapters, and in your own observations in your church and your community, you have undoubtedly seen dozens of ways that change is coming to our congregations. There will be many more changes that we cannot predict.

For those who have read my books and articles or listened to my conferences, webinars, and podcasts, you know I always want my audience to come away with a clear plan of action. In this concluding chapter, I offer some tangible changes I see on the horizon for churches. Though they aren't explicit action plans, they should immediately spark some ideas about how you can lead your church into the future.

Nine Key Changes for the Post-Quarantine Church

This list is by no means exhaustive. However, I hope it will be a starting point for you to continue to lead your post-quarantine church.

1. Simplicity Will Be Vitally Important

Do you remember how busy your church was before the pandemic? Do you remember how programs and ministries competed with one another for calendar space? Do you remember how weary your most committed church members were from trying to keep up and remain faithful to the congregation?

Perhaps you sensed that members who became inactive or dropped out altogether were struggling with church ministry burnout, though you may not specifically know their reasons.

And then the pandemic introduced a whole new set of challenges.

But maybe like a lot of pastors and church leaders I've spoken with, you noticed something else as well during the quarantine: You were able to slow down. You were able to focus on a few ministries instead of running yourself ragged trying to keep a lot of other plates spinning.

As you reflect on the pause we all experienced in the middle of a reset, please hear me well. One of the most harmful things you can do in the post-quarantine era is to allow your church to become too busy again. There will be a temptation—and maybe some overt pressure from certain members—to return to the complex church of the past. You may be tempted not only to return to earlier activities, but to add a layer of digital innovations on top.

Just say no.

Create a process to stringently evaluate everything new as well as every preexisting commitment of the congregation.

Healthy churches in the post-quarantine era will be focused churches. They will be congregations that do a few things well, both digitally and in person.

There is no time like the present to replace complexity with simplicity.

2. Only Outwardly Focused Churches Will Survive

This issue is far more important than a few words can capture. For years, many congregations have acted like religious country clubs. Members paid for services and got perks and benefits. Our team has worked with innumerable congregations where almost no effort was being made to obey the Great Commission.

These inwardly focused churches survived because they still had enough people who would attend and support the congregation simply because it was a cultural expectation. In many churches, that remnant disappeared almost completely during the pandemic.

The equation is simple. If churches are not making focused, intentional, and regular efforts to reach their communities, they will die.

3. Worship Service Gatherings Will Be Smaller

As I noted earlier in the book, the trend toward building larger worship centers to accommodate big congregations was primarily for one generation, the Boomers. What we are seeing now is a trend toward smaller gatherings. The presence and growth of neighborhood churches will play a major role in the post-quarantine era.

Of course, many churches were forced by social distancing requirements into smaller gatherings immediately after congregations began regathering. A number of churches added extra services and will keep them. Some will add even more. Some are becoming "multi" churches for the first time. Which brings us to the next change.

4. "Multi" Will Multiply

The post-quarantine era will see a rapid expansion of the "multi" movement in churches. For some churches, as noted above, that simply means holding multiple services on Sunday morning. But *multi* has other expressions as well.

The pandemic was the final straw for a lot of churches who decided they could no longer survive. But instead of closing their doors, they deeded their properties to other churches. As Sam Rainer has said, they were "adopted" by other congregations.[1] Those churches transitioned quickly into multisite churches.

Some churches recognized that a huge swath of the working population could not attend worship services on Sunday mornings, so they became multi by going to multiple days, creating worship services at alternative times beyond Sunday morning.

In response to social distancing, some churches recognized that not everyone had to gather in a dedicated worship center. So their attendees began meeting in overflow rooms, in fellowship halls, and in smaller chapels. In some cases, the additional space accommodated different language groups. These churches became multivenue.

The multi movement was already growing before the pandemic. It cannot be slowed in the post-quarantine era.

5. *Staff and Leadership Realignment Will Focus More on Digital Proficiency*

Watch for churches to allocate greater resources to digital technology and outreach. This shift is a natural one after so much attention was given to streaming worship services and transitioning to digital giving during the quarantine.

But this is about more than simply having the latest technological toy. What is happening now is an increased awakening to the reality that the digital world is a mission field—a way to reach real people with real needs. To meet this growing opportunity, churches will need to reallocate resources—including personnel. Young digital natives who are already technologically savvy will be the most in-demand for staff positions. Some will have "digital" in their ministry titles.

6. *"Stragglers" Will Become a Subject of Outreach and Focus*

I believe a new group of unchurched folks will emerge. For now, I will call them "stragglers." Before the pandemic, they were at least marginally involved with a church. But during the quarantine, they decided they preferred not attending church in person. When churches began to regather, the stragglers did not return.

Some stragglers will move to a digital-only connection with their churches. Others will completely drop out of church attendance.

Entire new strategies will be developed to reach the stragglers. New resources will be created. Church leaders will recognize this group as more receptive to the gospel and to reconnecting with the church than other unchurched people.

7. Digital Worship Services Will Be Newly Purposed

During the pandemic, two early trends emerged among churches. One was the move to digital giving. In response to a serious and growing concern about the financial sustainability of some church ministries, Church Answers dealt with hundreds of churches that had never made online giving available their members.

The second major trend was digital worship services. Church leaders, many of whom were a long way from being technologically savvy, figured out how to use platforms such as YouTube, Facebook, and Vimeo.

For most churches, digital worship services are still a mainstay among their post-quarantine ministries. Pastors realize they can reach people they would never reach in person. Church leaders are developing strategies that will make these services look significantly different in the future.

Churches also learned that digital worship services were useful for reaching their own members, many of whom could not attend otherwise. When a church in Florida specifically communicated with three retirement homes where some of their older members were homebound, they reaped the benefits of two unforeseen consequences. First, some of these senior adults invited their friends at the retirement home to watch the digital services, sometimes viewing them together.

Second, many of these members and guests started giving financially to the church. This particular Florida church saw giving increase more than 25 percent during the pandemic, most of it connected to the retirement homes.

8. Ministry Training Will Change Dramatically

For years, we have witnessed a significant shift in higher education as more students moved from on-campus enrollment to digital classes or a combination of both. Certainly, the world of theological and ministry training has seen that same shift.

Before the pandemic, the conversation was largely focused on delivery of education. For ministry training more specifically, the conversation focused on new digital models, along with cohort and church-based models.

While those discussions are still vital, a parallel issue has arisen. Not only is the *delivery* of ministry training or theological education changing, but so is the *content*. Certain parts of ministry training should always remain stable, such as New Testament, Old Testament, theology, church history, and other classical disciplines. But for the past several years, many church leaders have been asking for the theological content to be augmented with practical training, particularly in the various forms of leadership training. An entire cottage industry has since emerged, promising to train church leaders in the areas they did not learn in seminary or Bible college.

The pandemic generated an awareness of another major gap in most ministry training. Few church leaders have been trained or equipped to understand, engage in, or strategically plan for the digital world.

Ministry training was already changing before the pandemic. Watch for these changes to accelerate in the post-quarantine era.

9. Pastors Will Leave Their Lead Positions for Second-Chair Roles

The shift will likely be subtle at first, but we see signs of it unfolding already. Most pastors have not been trained or equipped for leading change on the scale needed for the post-quarantine era. As we noted earlier, they are typically trained well in the classical disciplines, but they are often ill-prepared for a world of fast-paced change.

Certainly, some will be prepared or will seek additional training. Some have more innate leadership skills to rely on. But many do not. This new era is daunting for even seasoned leaders.

Meanwhile, a parallel movement is growing. As more churches join the multi movement, they will be seeking ministers for new sites, venues, and campuses. A number of seasoned pastors will fit these more-limited roles well. I'm calling them second-chair roles, because although they will still be pastoral in nature, they will not include the specific leadership responsibilities of a lead pastor.

The Blank Slate Church

The post-quarantine era may prove to be one of the most challenging seasons for churches and their leaders. The opportunity to lead change is likely greater than at any other point in our lifetimes. Without a doubt, the world has changed. Without a doubt, Western culture has shifted; and it has shifted largely against churches. Without a doubt, most church leaders have not been trained and equipped for this new season.

Still, it is a season of opportunity. In some ways, it is like a blank slate. One pastor stated it succinctly and well: "I feel like I'm back in my church planting days," he said. "I really need to lead my church to start over in most areas. I am both excited and nervous."

This book has introduced you to some of the challenges most churches will face in the post-quarantine era. But there is so much more we don't know yet. There is much more change on the path ahead.

I can only imagine how the first-century Christians felt as they were trying to reach a world that needed to hear the good news of the resurrected Savior. I can only imagine their excitement and their fear. They knew the path ahead would be both difficult and dangerous. But they also knew their efforts would be worth the cost.

As we enter this unknown era, we're uncertain about the specifics of what will unfold, but we remain certain that the God of all wisdom and power will be with us every step of the way. After Jesus gave his disciples the Great Commission mandate in Matthew 28:19-20, he reminded them that they were not going it alone: "Be sure of this: I am with you always, even to the end of the age."[2]

With that same assurance, we enter a new era, a new season of opportunity. With that same promise, we lead our churches into the future. And with that same confidence, we know we will not be alone, regardless of what unfolds.

When it's all said and done, nothing else really matters.

NOTES

CHALLENGE 1:
GATHER DIFFERENTLY AND BETTER

1. Hebrews 10:24
2. Hebrews 10:25

CHALLENGE 2:
SEIZE YOUR OPPORTUNITY TO REACH THE DIGITAL WORLD

1. Alex Petros, "Acquisitions in the Time of COVID: Big Tech Gets Bigger," Public Knowledge, April 7, 2020, https:// www.publicknowledge.org/blog/acquisitions-in-the-time-of -covid-big-tech-gets-bigger/; Drew Singer and Elena Popina, "Apple, Alphabet Still Buying Back Shares as Tech Giants Flush with Cash," Bloomberg News, April 30, 2020, https:// www.bnnbloomberg.ca/apple-alphabet-still-buying-back-shares -as-tech-giants-flush-with-cash-1.1429737.
2. Acts 1:8
3. Acts 1:14
4. Luke 10:2

CHALLENGE 3:
RECONNECT WiTH THE COMMUNITY NEAR YOUR CHURCH
1. Acts 1:8
2. Acts 8:1

CHALLENGE 4:
TAKE PRAYER TO A NEW AND POWERFUL LEVEL
1. Acts 1:14
2. Acts 6:1
3. Acts 6:4
4. Acts 6:7
5. Evan Andrews, "8 Ways Roads Helped Rome Rule the Ancient World," History.com, August 29, 2018, https://www.history .com/news/8-ways-roads-helped-rome-rule-the-ancient-world; *Encyclopaedia Brittanica Online*, s.v. "Roman Road System," accessed June 20, 2020, https://www.britannica.com/technology /Roman-road-system; *World Heritage Encyclopedia*, s.v. "Roman Road," accessed June 20, 20202, http://www.self.gutenberg .org/articles/eng/Roman_road#cite_note-Corbishley.2C_Mike _page_50-4.
6. See, for example, Clea Simon, "Is Technology Evil?" *Harvard Gazette*, October 3, 2019, https://news.harvard.edu/gazette/story /2019/10/hubweek-panel-explores-ethics-in-the-digital-world/; David Brooks, "How Evil Is Tech?" *New York Times*, November 20, 2017, https://www.nytimes.com/2017/11/20/opinion/how -evil-is-tech.html; Kathleen Stansberry, Janna Anderson, and Lee Rainie, "Experts Optimistic About the Next 50 Years of Digital Life," Pew Research Center, October 28, 2019, https:// www.pewresearch.org/internet/2019/10/28/experts-optimistic -about-the-next-50-years-of-digital-life/; Chelsea Greenwood, "9 Subtle Ways Technology Is Making Humanity Worse," Business Insider, August 23, 2019, https://www.businessinsider .com/technology-negative-bad-effects-society-2019-8.
7. Acts 6:1
8. Acts 6:3, 5-6
9. Acts 6:7

CHALLENGE 5:
RETHINK YOUR FACILITIES FOR EMERGING OPPORTUNITIES

1. See, for example, Cheryl Mitchell Gaines and Chelsea Langston Bombino, "Why the Black Church Is Vital for Healthy Communities," *Public Justice Review* 6 (2017), http://www.sharedjustice .org/domestic-justice/2017/12/20/why-the-black-church-is-vital -for-healthy-communities; Bob Osborne, "Why Don't Churches Share?" EFCA blog, August 20, 2018, https://www.efca.org /blog/leading-churches/why-dont-churches-share; Jim Morgan, "10 Ways Churches Underutilize Their Facilities," Meet the Need, November 1, 2017, http://meettheneed.org/blog/2017/11 /10-ways-churches-underutilize-facilities/.

2. US Bureau of Labor Statistics, "American Time Use Survey—2018 Results," news release no. USDL-19-1003, June 19, 2019, https:// www.bls.gov/news.release/pdf/atus.pdf.

CHALLENGE 6:
MAKE LASTING CHANGES THAT WILL MAKE A DIFFERENCE

1. See Acts 1:14; 2:42; 6:4; 12:12; 13:3; 14:23.
2. Hebrews 11:8-10
3. Stephen Kendrick and Alex Kendrick, *The Love Dare* (Nashville: B&H Publishing, 2008).

CONCLUDING THOUGHTS:
FROM CHALLENGES TO OPPORTUNITIES

1. Thom Rainer and Sam Rainer, "A Case Study of an Established Church Adopting a Struggling Church," *Rainer on Leadership* podcast, episode 576, October 1, 2019, 5:14–10:49, https:// churchanswers.com/podcasts/rainer-on-leadership/a-case-study -of-an-established-church-adopting-a-struggling-church-rainer -on-leadership-576/. See also Jessica Pigg, "Bradenton Church Commits to Help Dying Churches," Florida Baptist Convention, September 23, 2019, https://flbaptist.org/bradenton-church -commits-to-help-dying-churches/.

2. Matthew 28:20

ABOUT THE AUTHOR

Thom S. Rainer is founder and CEO of Church Answers. With nearly forty years of ministry experience, Thom has spent a lifetime committed to the growth and health of the local church and its leaders. Prior to  founding Church Answers, Thom served as president and CEO of LifeWay Christian Resources. Before LifeWay, he served at the Southern Baptist Theological Seminary for twelve years, where he was the founding dean of the Billy Graham School of Missions, Evangelism, and Ministry. He is a 1977 graduate of the University of Alabama and earned his master of divinity and PhD from the Southern Baptist Theological Seminary. In addition to speaking in hundreds of venues over the past thirty years, Thom led Rainer Group, a church and denominational consulting firm that provided church health insights to more than five hundred churches and other organizations from 1990 to 2005. Thom is the author of more than two dozen books. He and his wife, Nellie Jo, live in Nashville.